PITCH CORRECTION SOFTWARE NOW!

PITCH CORRECTION SOFTWARE NOW!

Max Mobley

Hal Leonard Books
An Imprint of Hal Leonard Corporation

Published in 2013 by Hal Leonard Books
An Imprint of Hal Leonard Corporation
7777 West Bluemound Road
Milwaukee, WI 53213

Trade Book Division Editorial Offices
33 Plymouth St., Montclair, NJ 07042

Printed in the United States of America
Book design by Kristina Rolander

Library of Congress Cataloging-in-Publication Data
Mobley, Max.
 Pitch correction software now! / Max Mobley.
    pages cm
 Includes index.
 1. Auto-tune (Computer file) 2. T-Pain Effect (Computer file) 3. Nectar (Computer file) 4. Waves Tune (Computer file) 5. Melodyne (Computer file) 6. Computer sound processing. I. Title.
 ML74.3.M63 2013
 781.49'028553--dc23

                              2012047470

ISBN 978-1-4768-1418-6

www.halleonardbooks.com

CONTENTS

ACKNOWLEDGMENTS

» Greg Ondo, field marketing manager for Steinberg GmbH.

» Derk Hagedorn

» Anders Steele

» Bill Gibson, developmental editor at Hal Leonard Books

» In-tune and out-of-tune vocals provided by Tina Davey

» Music provided by Bobby "One-Sock" Templin

» Additional music provided by The Cranks of Santa Cruz, California, with vocals by Mike Hilden.

» Special thanks to Antares, Waves, iZotope, and Celemony for licenses and support of their excellent pitch correction software.

PITCH CORRECTION SOFTWARE NOW!

1 MODERN PITCH CORRECTION

Modern pitch correction software has been around since 1997, when Antares Audio Technologies introduced the original Auto-Tune plug-in for Digidesign Pro Tools. For many years, Auto-Tune was the only game in town, and many professionals still consider it the gold standard. Technology has evolved rapidly over the past 15 years (just compare today's computers and cell phones with those from the late 1990s, for example), and today's music maker has many different pitch correction options available.

iZotope has become a pitch correction powerhouse with its Nectar and star-powered The T-Pain Effect software products. Waves, within its vast line of pro audio plug-ins, offers Waves Tune and a lite version, Waves Tune LT. And Celemony Software's Grammy Award–winning Melodyne Editor has redefined the technology by offering polyphonic pitch correction coupled with sophisticated time and rhythm editing, thereby extending its use beyond mere vocals and monophonic audio.

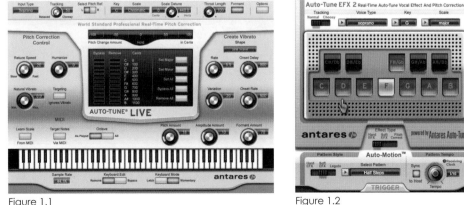

Figure 1.1   Figure 1.2

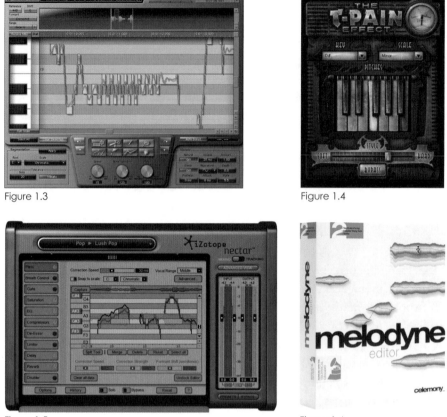

Figure 1.3

Figure 1.4

Figure 1.5

Figure 1.6

At last count, including lite and bundled versions, there are over 15 different pitch correction software products vying for your dollars at local music stores. Prices range from about $50 to more than $500. Each one has its strengths and weaknesses, depending on your workflow, musical style, and production goals. And if the types of music and artists you deal with vary from project to project, having just one pitch correction solution may not be enough. Deciding which pitch correction tool (or tools) is right for you and your studio may not be easy. Nonetheless, if the music you make contains vocals, then some form of pitch correction belongs in your studio toolkit.

This book looks closely at the most innovative and popular pitch correction titles available today. The concepts and features are presented in a way that helps musicians and producers of all levels apply this technology quickly and with highly professional results.

PITCH CORRECTION TOOLS VERSUS VOCAL EFFECTS

Pitch correction software functions as a tool for repairing pitch problems in vocal tracks and as a distinct and recognizable vocal effect. Although the two tasks are very different processes, both can be accomplished using the same software. The term *transparent pitch correction* refers to using the technology to put or keep musical parts (usually, but not exclusively, vocals) in tune. In such instances, listeners are not even aware that it has been applied. Instead, they just hear vocals and music that are fully in tune.

Using the same technology as a vocal effect requires applying pitch-related signal processing to a vocal part in a very obvious and prominent manner (as opposed to the transparency associated with pitch correction as a tool). Many people refer to this effect as "Auto-Tuning," or as the "Cher effect" or "T-Pain effect," since it was first heard on Cher's 1998 hit "Believe" and has since become the signature sound of rapper T-Pain, who now has his own brand of the technology produced in partnership with iZotope. Use of this effect in the music you make should influence your decision on which pitch correction product (or products) you buy.

REAL-TIME VERSUS OFFLINE (MANUAL) PITCH CORRECTION

Pitch correction, like many other digital audio processes, can occur in a real-time (online) or an offline (manually applied and not in real time) environment. Just like the various applications of pitch correction itself, both have their place.

REAL-TIME PITCH CORRECTION

Real-time mode is exactly what it sounds like—using pitch correction live, whether on stage or during the mixing phase of a recording project. Set the key and the scale, turn off any notes you do not want the program to correct to, adjust correction speed to taste (more on this later), and then hit Play or start singing. With certain lite versions, such as Auto-Tune EFX 2, all you need to do is set the key and scale and decide if you want transparent correction or a vocal effect. The rest is done for you—and yes, it can be that easy to get professional results.

Figure 1.7

PITCH CORRECTION LIVE

Given the current standard of what it means to sing in tune (thanks to the ubiquitous use of pitch correction over the past decade), along with the strain that gigging can put on a singer's voice, using real-time pitch correction has become requisite for many live acts. And for live performance, dedicated hardware remains popular. This is due in large part to the complexities and latency involved with adding to the live mix, a computer running a digital audio workstation (DAW) such as Pro Tools or Cubase, which is in turn running one instance of a pitch correction plug-in per vocal needing correction. Even Antares's Auto-Tune Live, which is optimized for live use, runs only as a DAW plug-in. However, computers are commonplace on today's stages big and small, and so is pitch correction software running on those computers.

While the focus of this book is on studio use, where pitch correction is used both online and offline, the myriad online and real-time tips and tricks offered in this book can easily be applied to using the technology on stage. It's also worth noting that of the different pitch correction titles covered in this book, only iZotope's The T-Pain Engine offers real-time pitch correction as a standalone program.

Real-time pitch correction in the studio is a bit of a misnomer, since vocals are rarely recorded with an effect or other process on them (though they may be monitored with effects such as reverb and delay). Recording a vocal track with effects also interferes with the pitch detection phase of the pitch correction process—so just don't do it!

OFFLINE/GRAPHICAL/MANUAL MODE

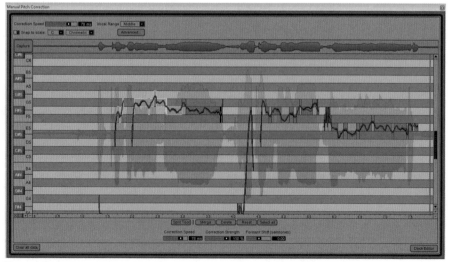

Figure 1.8

Offline or graphical mode (graph mode for short) means you have to record or import into the software the audio you wish to apply pitch correction to, and then manually edit pitch on a note-by-note, word-by-word, or section-by-section basis. In this mode, pitch edits are performed manually on a graph showing notes on the vertical axis and time on the horizontal axis. Manipulating objects used for defining the shape, value, and placement of corrected pitches is the primary focus of manual pitch correction. This manual mode is where pitch correction software really flexes its muscle. It is a great mode for transparent pitch correction (it offers surgically precise control over the correction process) and for a vocal effect (manipulating melody and creating effects is highly intuitive and very powerful).

Many professional engineers and producers work in this mode because of its power and flexibility. Programs such as Celemony Melodyne and Waves Tune offer only a graphical mode, though they remain in sync with the project and edits can be heard during playback. Auto-Tune and Nectar support both real-time and offline modes.

Real-time or graphical environments, polyphonic versus monophonic pitch correction (monophonic = a single voice; polyphonic = multiple voices such as a guitar or piano chord), as well as other workflow methodologies covered in later chapters are key pieces to the puzzle when incorporating pitch correction into your audio production. But they are not the only factors. Fortunately, every pitch correction title covered in this book is available to try before you buy. That's an essential step to making any informed software purchase.

2 ANTARES AUTO-TUNE:
THE GRANDFATHER OF PITCH CORRECTION TECHNOLOGY

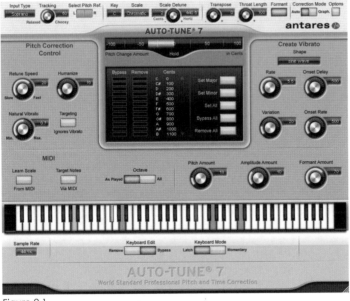

Figure 2.1

Antares Audio Technologies' first version of Auto-Tune came out in the late 1990s, and the world of popular Western music has never been the same. Auto-Tune 7 is Antares's flagship version as of this writing. Its cousins, Auto-Tune Evo and Auto-Tune Live, are largely identical in how they work. Therefore, many of the concepts and workflow discussed with regard to Auto-Tune 7 will also apply to Auto-Tune Evo and Auto-Tune Live.

AUTO-TUNE 7 DETAILS

» **Format: AU, VST, RTAS, TDM**

» **License System: iLok**

» **Price: $399 (Native), $649 (TDM)**

AUTOMATIC (AUTO) MODE PITCH CORRECTION IN AUTO-TUNE

Auto-Tune's Automatic mode (Auto mode for short) operates in real time. As audio is played through the plug-in, pitch correction is applied and output. Auto mode is fast and intuitive. It offers professional results and a speedy workflow.

AUTO MODE PITCH CORRECTION PARAMETERS

Here's a look at Auto-Tune Auto mode's frequently used parameters.

Input Type

Setting the Input Type focuses Auto-Tune's pitch detection process to specific frequencies or pitches. When you are working with vocal parts that have a wide pitch range, or when you are uncertain what setting to use, Alto/Tenor Voice is a great place to start.

The following are Auto-Tune's various Input Type settings:

» Soprano

» Alto/Tenor

» Low Male

» Instrument

» Bass Instrument

Figure 2.2

Tracking

The Tracking parameter controls how selective Auto-Tune will be in detecting pitches in the source audio that will subsequently be corrected. This is an important function, since pitch detection must occur before pitch correction can take place. The default is 50, which is halfway between its maximum settings for Relaxed and Choosy. Auto-Tune's pitch detection technology has improved so much over the years that adjusting this parameter should be a rare event. However, if you find Auto-Tune is not detecting notes or parts sufficiently, and the key and scale are set correctly as described below, then tweaking this knob may help.

Key and Scale

When you click on the Key and Scale parameters in Auto-Tune, menus will appear allowing you to select the best key and scale for your project and the audio being processed. Notes from this selection will be shown in the Edit Scale display described below.

Auto-Tune offers 29 different scales including chromatic, which includes all notes regardless of selected key. If your source material is sharp or flat by only a few cents, or less than half a semitone, than setting Scale to chromatic can yield good results since this will correct all pitches to the closest half step (1 half step = 1 semitone).

Figure 2.3

Target Notes

In Auto mode, Auto-Tune corrects pitch based on Target notes, which are established by the Key and Scale settings. They appear inside the Edit Scale display, which is described below. As you will soon see, they can be manipulated.

Scale Detune

All scales and keys in Auto mode assume the reference pitch of A4 = 440 Hz. This means that all keys are based on A above middle C being tuned to 440 Hz, or 440 cycles per second—the standard reference pitch for most Western music. If the music accompanying the tracks needing pitch correction does not conform to the A4 = 440 Hz reference pitch, use the Scale Detune knob to adjust Auto-Tune's scales and keys to the reference pitch of your music. The range of this parameter is plus or minus 100 cents (100 cents = 1 semitone).

Transpose

Whereas Scale Detune changes the reference pitch of the scales and keys that Auto-Tune uses for pitch correction, Transpose changes the pitch, by semitones,

Figure 2.4

of the source audio itself. Transpose adjustments usually require engaging the Formant button to preserve the transposed audio's formants.

Formant

Turn on Formant Correction to keep large changes in pitch (usually a full step or greater) sounding natural. Without formant correction, large changes in pitch can sound unrealistic.

Throat Length

Auto-Tune's Throat Length control lets you modify the characteristics of a vocal performance by adjusting the length of a throat model included in Auto-Tune. To engage Throat Length you must first click on the Formant button.

Pitch Change Amount Indicator

This meter shows how much pitch correction is being applied.

Figure 2.5

Edit Scale Display

This window shows you the Target notes defined by the selected Key and Scale, and gives you control over them. Each Target note shown in this window can be bypassed or removed from the scale by clicking on its respective Bypass or Remove button. For any nondiatonic scale, Set Major and Set Minor buttons will also appear here. Let's take a look at these controls.

Figure 2.6

» **Bypass.** Setting a Target note to Bypass will cause original pitches close to that note to be ignored and pass through unprocessed by Auto-Tune.

» **Remove.** Removed notes are removed from the current scale, forcing Auto-Tune to correct to the next closest note in that scale. For example, if you remove F♯ from an E minor scale, then any notes close to F♯ will be corrected to G if sharper than F♯, or E if flatter than F♯.

» **Bypass All and Remove All.** Clicking on either of these will bypass or remove all Target notes in the currently selected scale, which you can then select on a per-note basis by clicking on an individual note's Bypass or Remove button.

» **Set Major and Set Minor.** Clicking on either of these will remove all notes of the currently selected key and scale that are not part of a major or minor scale.

» **Set All.** Click on Set All to reset Bypass and Remove filters.

All adjustments in the Edit Scale display affect all octaves. To focus edits to a specific octave, use the Virtual Keyboard at the bottom of the Auto-Tune Auto mode window.

VIRTUAL KEYBOARD, KEYBOARD EDIT, AND KEYBOARD MODE

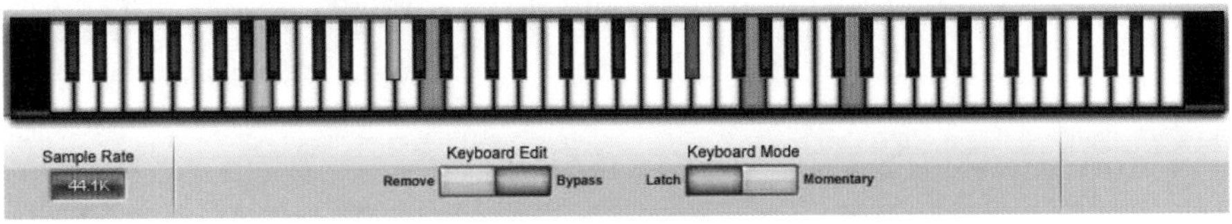

Figure 2.7

When audio is running through Auto mode, keys on its virtual keyboard turn blue to show the detected incoming pitches—a great reference for helping you find the key and scale of your music if you do not know them. Keys here can also be clicked on in order to bypass or remove notes in the selected scale. Whether selected notes are removed or bypassed here depends on the Keyboard Edit setting.

The Virtual Keyboard is available for editing only when a 12-note scale is selected from the Scale menu. If you wish to edit a major or minor scale (both have less than 12 notes), choose a chromatic scale and then click on the Set Major or Set Minor buttons inside the Edit Scale display.

The Virtual Keyboard uses color coding to reveal the state of any key. Notes in the current scale will keep their traditional white or black colors.

Virtual Keyboard Color Codes

» **Blue.** Detected pitches of the source audio.

» **Gray.** Notes removed from the scale.

» **Brown.** Notes bypassed from the scale.

THE PITCH CORRECTION CONTROL SECTION

Pitch correction as a tool and as an effect is primarily determined by adjustments in the Pitch Correction Control section. Here's a tour of important parameters found in this section:

Figure 2.8

» **Retune Speed.** This parameter controls how fast pitch correction is applied, and is therefore largely responsible for delivering both transparent pitch correction and the Auto-Tune vocal effect. Values are in milliseconds, from zero to 400.

» **Humanize.** This parameter applies a slower retune speed to longer notes, allowing the nuances of the performance to come through while helping to keep the pitch correction process highly transparent. Values range from zero (off) to 100.

» **Natural Vibrato.** The Natural Vibrato knob works on vibrato present in the performance being pitch-corrected. Its function is to decrease or increase the width of that vibrato (width = the distance between a vibrato's low and high pitches). Its default state is zero (off).

» **Targeting Ignores Vibrato.** Auto-Tune can sometimes attempt to pitch-correct wide vibrato performances to two different notes. This can cause an unnatural warbling sound. Engaging this feature often helps, and when it doesn't, manual pitch correction to the rescue!

TRANSPARENT PITCH CORRECTION IN AUTO MODE

Using Auto mode is a fast and easy way to apply highly professional pitch correction to your track. Set the appropriate key and scale, bypass or remove notes in the Edit Scale display, turn on the Formant button, and you are largely done. But wait, there is one more knob that deserves your attention.

THE POWER OF RETUNE SPEED

As mentioned previously, this control sets how quickly pitch correction will be applied to the audio being processed by Auto-Tune. When set to zero, pitch correction is quantized to exact notes, and in the process, subtle changes in pitch that are a key component of singing are removed, thus giving the well-known effect made famous by T-Pain, Cher, and many others. That's right, achieving this effect can be as simple as turning Auto-Tune's Retune Speed knob to 0. For transparent pitch correction, experiment with settings between 25 and 100 milliseconds. Try higher settings for ballad and slow-tempo numbers. Let your ears be the judge.

THE AUTO-TUNE EFFECT IN AUTO MODE

Set Retune Speed and Humanize to 0, and turn on Formant Correction. That's it for the most part. But read on for some tips on working with this effect.

AUTO-TUNE EFFECT TIPS AND TRICKS

A common complaint when working with the Auto-Tune effect is that even at 0 Retune Speed, the effect is not prominent enough. The reason for this is simple. The greater the difference between source pitch and output pitch, the more prominent the Auto-Tune effect will be. So if Auto-Tune is moving notes by less than a semitone, it stands to reason that the Auto-Tune effect will not be very prominent. When this happens there are a few solutions available.

CHANGE KEYS FOR A PROMINENT EFFECT

If you know in advance that the Auto-Tune effect will be employed in the project, record the vocal destined for the effect in a different key or octave than what the final version of the project requires. Use Auto mode's scale and pitch parameters to bring the vocal back to the correct scale and key. This allows Auto-Tune to perform pitch quantization to a higher degree, thus making the effect more prominent. When going this route, do the vocalist a favor by changing the key of the music during tracking so they can sing in the "wrong" key easily. For most electronic music, changing keys is trivial.

LESS REALLY CAN BE MORE

Now that the Auto-Tune effect has become a mainstay of pop vocal production (as well as country, reggae, and rock), using the effect at its most prominent may make your song sound run-of-the-mill and not stand out. Customize your version of the effect by dialing up Retune Speed (anywhere between 0 and 12 can be effective), applying it just to certain passages, and experimenting with different Target notes by removing or bypassing some, either for the whole track or just certain parts. In other words, make the effect your own.

AUTO MODE AND MIDI

Auto-Tune's Auto mode allows you to define Target note scales via MIDI. This works great when you're working with the Auto-Tune effect and you want to augment melody. For this to work at all, your DAW must be able to route MIDI data to audio plug-ins. Most of the major DAWs do this easily (consult your DAW manual for details).

HOW TO USE MIDI WITH AUTO MODE

This walk-through focuses on Auto mode's Learn Scale From MIDI feature. It can also be applied to Auto mode's Target Notes Via MIDI. The key differences here are that "Learn Scale" establishes a scale that can be saved and recalled, and "Target Notes" does not—once the MIDI data has stopped being sent to Auto-Tune, Target Notes are no longer available.

1. With your MIDI keyboard or MIDI track routed to Auto-Tune, click on the Learn Scale From MIDI button. When engaged it will light up blue, all the keys shown in the virtual keyboard will be grayed out, and the notes shown in the Edit Scale display will be set to Remove.

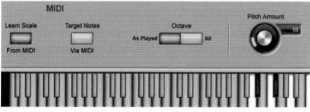

Figure 2.9

2. Play a vocal part through Auto mode, along with the MIDI notes you wish to pitch-correct. As this happens, keys on Auto-Tune's Virtual Keyboard will turn white or black based on those MIDI notes.

You have just defined for Auto-Tune the scale it will use for pitch correction based on MIDI information. If Octave All was set for this, the scale is established for all octaves and can be saved as an Auto-Tune preset using your DAW's plug-in Preset dialog box (you must also save your project).

USING AUTO-TUNE'S GRAPHICAL MODE

The Graphical mode (Graph mode for short) found in Auto-Tune 7 and Auto-Tune Evo offers a high degree of precision over the pitch correction process, whether the goal is an effect or transparent pitch correction.

AUTO-TUNE GRAPHICAL MODE HOUSEKEEPING

Auto-Tune requires a buffer size setting in its Options window that matches or exceeds the audio being tracked into Graph mode. The default setting is 240 seconds, or four minutes. If you plan on tracking more than four minutes of audio into Graph mode, click on the Options button on the upper right of Auto-Tune and enter an appropriate buffer size. If you are tracking less than four minutes of audio, it is safe to leave this parameter at its default setting.

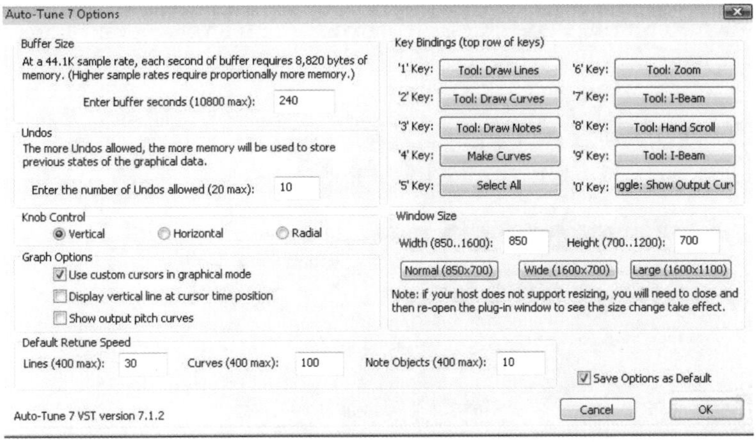

Figure 2.10

For Graphical mode playback to sync properly with your DAW and be fully supported by your DAW's transport controls, Auto-Tune needs to receive valid project clock information from that DAW. Most DAWs do this automatically. In Graphical mode, Source should be set to Host (the default setting) in such cases. A quick way to check if valid clock information is being sent to Auto-Tune is to, with Host selected, use your DAW's play and stop controls. If the cursor inside of Graph mode's Pitch Graph display starts, moves, and stops in accordance with your DAW, then you're good to go. If not, set Source to

Internal, which forces you to have to start playback at the exact same place you started tracking audio into Graph mode, and to use Graph mode's Reset button to stop playback. In Internal Source mode, rendering or mixing down Auto-Tune processing requires Auto-Tune to be open and visible.

Figure 2.11

WORKING INSIDE THE PITCH GRAPH DISPLAY

This window inside of Graph mode is where tracked audio will appear for pitch editing. It is shown behind pitch reference lines stemming from the display's vertical axis, and timelines in bars and beats or seconds stemming from the display's horizontal axis. Both axes have typical scroll, plus, and minus zoom buttons to move around the Pitch Graph display and to manage what reference note lines are visible. Horizontal movements move only what audio is visible in this display. Vertical movements move only what reference pitch lines are visible in the display. The workflow concept here is that pitch correction objects are placed inside the Pitch Graph display based on those time and note lines. Each of these objects can be moved, or its contour changed. Each can also have its own Retune Speed values, giving you a high level of control over the pitch correction process.

USING AUTO MODE TO ACCELERATE GRAPH MODE PITCH CORRECTION

Figure 2.12

Starting in Automatic mode and then moving over to Graphical mode offers a speedy workflow.

1. With Auto-Tune placed on an audio insert on the track requiring pitch correction, use Auto mode's Key, Scale, and Retune Speed parameters to dial in pitch correction to taste, while leaving all other parameters turned off or set to null. Also bypass or remove any Target notes as needed. Since you'll soon be hopping over to Graph mode, Auto mode pitch correction doesn't need to be set perfectly—you just want to get it close. Play back the audio until you are familiar with how it sounds being processed with the current Auto mode settings. Once you are happy with these settings, click on the Graph mode button and enter Graph mode.

2. Return your transport to the point where you wish to begin tracking audio into Graph mode for manual pitch correction. Always begin tracking on a silent part of the audio, otherwise glitches can occur at that starting point. Press the Track Pitch button, causing it to flash red and blue, letting you know that Graph mode is armed and ready for audio capture. Press Play on your DAW's transport. This initiates recording into Graph mode. An ideal way to work in Auto-Tune's Graph mode is to track (record) in the entire audio track, even if you are applying pitch correction to only a portion of it. Once all the audio is tracked, stop playback. You should now see an amplitude waveform inside the Pitch Graph display, along with a series of Red Input Pitch Curves, which reflect pitches detected but not yet corrected by Auto-Tune. Use the vertical and horizontal zoom buttons so that you can see all of the tracked audio and most or all of the red curves. If Auto Scroll is engaged, this happens automatically.

   Green Output Pitch Curves may be visible at this time. These curves provide a visual reference of the final output pitch. While this can be helpful, it can also clutter up the Pitch Graph display, so hide them by going to the Options window and deselecting Show Output Pitch Curves. Now is a good time to assign a key on your QWERTY keyboard to show and hide these curves. Use the Key Bindings section in the Options window, and on a key of your choosing select Toggle: Show Output Curve.

3. Click on the Import Auto button. This places Blue Correction Curves across the entire track based on Auto mode's settings, including Key and Scale, and the location of the red curves. These blue curves are applying pitch correction to your track. If you had highlighted a region in Graph mode, then blue curves would have been placed within that region only.

When using the Import Auto function, the default Retune Speeds set in the Options dialog box will override Retune Speed values set in Auto mode. Because of this, you may need to adjust Retune Speed for the newly created blue curves, as described below.

4. Play back the audio and listen to the results. It should sound the same as in Auto mode. You can now use Graph mode's tools to surgically edit pitch by changing the shape, placement, and length of those blue curves and their individual Retune Speeds.

5. When Correction objects are selected, the per-object Retune Speed control located beneath the Pitch Graph display becomes available. This control allows you to set a different Retune Speed for each existing Correction object (in this case, blue curves). This goes far in dialing in highly transparent pitch correction. Once again, let your ears be your guide. Now is a good time to experiment with this control. Select a specific blue curve by clicking on it with the Arrow tool (select the Arrow tool above the Pitch Graph display if it is not already selected), and then adjust its per-object Retune Speed. Retune Speed can also be set for groups of Correction objects. Use the Arrow tool and drag left or right, thus creating a region of selected blue curves.

   To keep large changes in pitch natural sounding, make sure that the Formant Correction button is turned on!

6. Let's use the Arrow tool to move blue curves as needed to perfect the application of transparent pitch correction.

   Select the Arrow tool if it is not already selected, and use it to click on a blue curve you wish to edit. To move an entire blue curve vertically to a new pitch, click in the middle of it and drag it to the new location. Once the curve is selected, its start and end anchor points, shown as small black squares, will be visible. Click on one of these and drag to move the start or end of the curve in time (horizontally) or in pitch (vertically), thus changing the contour and start and end points of the curve. Play back the audio between edits to hear the results and guide the editing process.

   To make horizontal movements of curves or their anchor points, hold down the Control (Windows) or Option (Mac) key on your computer keyboard. Horizontal movements are constrained by adjacent Correction objects. Horizontal movements of blue curves are not recommended, since the curve's contour will be shifted away from the subtle modulations that formed their shape.

Output pitch is derived from Correction object location, shape, and their per-object parameters. Bring back those Green Output Pitch Curves for a visual reference of the output pitch based on your curve edits (including Retune Speed settings). A great way to grasp how Retune Speed affects output pitch is to watch the green curves while adjusting the per-object Retune Speed knob. Blue curves and output pitch curves will not always match because of these per-object parameters.

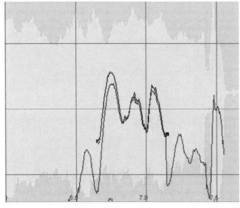

Figure 2.13

In order to understand the editing power at your fingertips, experiment with editing blue curves (including their Retune Speeds) while listening to your edits and studying related output pitch curves. Longer blue curves may require slower Retune Speeds, and shorter ones may require faster Retune Speeds. Dialing in Retune Speed on a per–Correction object basis as needed is key to highly transparent pitch correction.

When editing curves or any other Correction objects, zooming in ahead of time will improve editing precision.

GRAPH MODE AND THE AUTO-TUNE EFFECT

Auto-Tune's Graph mode is a great environment for working with the Auto-Tune effect and re-creating melody. Line objects, which must be drawn manually, and Note objects, which can be created automatically or drawn by hand, are both powerful Correction objects for such purposes.

USING NOTE OBJECTS FOR EFFECT AND MELODY WORK

1. Track into Graphical mode a vocal part that is 15 to 20 seconds long. Turn on Formant Correction, and also select Show Lanes (to the left of the Envelope Graph display). Doing so replaces pitch reference lines with lanes, which are ideal for Note objects. Using bars and beats as a time reference in your project will help here, assuming that your DAW is sending valid project time to the plug-in and that the timing of your song is based on the project's bars and beats time reference.

2. Adjust the Pitch Graph display so that all of the tracked audio is shown, along with as many red curves as possible.

3. Select the Note tool and draw a single Note object that covers the entire audio track. Set the per-object Retune Speed for this long Note object to 0.

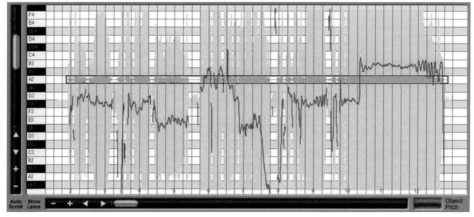

Figure 2.14

4. Select the Scissors tool and use it to cut up this single Note object into multiple objects of differing lengths. It doesn't really matter where you make your cuts at this point, since you will be changing them with ease later. Cutting them on the bars and beats lines of the Pitch Graph display is a very musical choice, assuming that they match the bars and beats of your project (they should).

5. Use the Arrow tool to move Note objects to different pitches. With Snap to Note turned on, Note objects will snap to the pitch you move them to. Zoom in on specific sections of audio when editing Note objects, since the Arrow tool's functionality changes based on where on a Note object it is. Near the ends of Note objects, it can be used to shorten or lengthen the object by clicking-and-dragging horizontally; in the middle, it is set to

grab them and move them vertically to different pitches. Remember that to move objects horizontally, you need to hold down Control (Windows) or Option (Mac).

If you have a melody in mind, move the Note objects to accommodate that melody. If you don't, move them to different notes at random—though, for the sake of simplicity, keep those moves well within an octave.

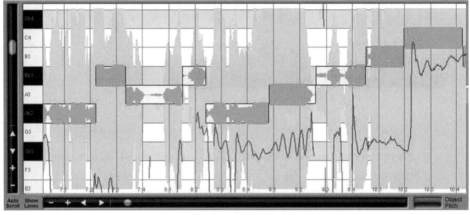

Figure 2.15

6. Play back the audio to hear the results. You should now hear a classic example of the Auto-Tune/Cher/T-Pain effect—probably with unusual timing and melody, unless you were lucky with your random cuts and movements or had edited Note objects with a melody in mind.

Listen to the results, and it should become obvious which Note objects require editing to tighten up those random cuts and pitches into a solid melody.

Instead of drawing a single, long Note object in the above walk-through, you could have used the Make Notes button and Number of Note Objects knob. Experiment with this method of Note object creation—it's highly intuitive.

LINE CORRECTION OBJECTS

Try the above walk-through using Line objects. This time click on the Line tool and use it to draw multiple Line objects at the pitches you wish to correct to or use in the melody. (Don't forget to adjust their Retune

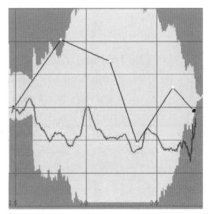

Figure 2.16

Speeds!) When creating Line objects, the first click starts the line, subsequent single-clicks create anchor points that define line segments, and a double-click terminates the line. Line anchors and termination points can be manipulated up and down and at various angles across different pitches with the Arrow tool. When Snap to Note is on, Line objects can be drawn only on note lines that pertain to the current scale.

AUTO-TUNE GRAPH MODE'S TOOLS

Figure 2.17

Here's a look at the tools most commonly used inside the Pitch Graph display.

» **Correction Object Drawing Tools (Line tool, Curve tool, and Note tool)**

Each of Auto-Tune's Correction objects has its own tool for drawing it inside the Pitch Graph display. Since you can have only one Correction object in a single location, though all three types can be used across the track at your discretion, drawing a Correction object always replaces any existing Correction objects in the same time location.

Figure 2.18

» **The Magnifying Glass (Zoom) Tool**

Click, hold, and drag around an area in the Pitch Graph display with the Magnifying Glass tool to focus and zoom in on that selected area. Single-click to zoom in one step (if not already at maximum zoom) and center the clicked point. Hold down the Control key (Windows) or Option key (Mac) while single-clicking to zoom out one step.

Figure 2.19

» **The I-Beam Tool**

Use this tool to highlight a section of audio in which you wish to use Graph mode's automatic settings such as Import Auto or Make Notes. Selecting a region with this tool also selects any Correction objects in that region. This allows you to set per-object parameters to groups of Correction objects.

Figure 2.20

Double-clicking anywhere in the Pitch Graph display with the I-Beam tool will select all of the audio tracked into Graph mode.

» **The Scissors Tool**

This tool can cut Correction objects into smaller objects, as shown in the Note object walk-through. This allows for more surgical pitch editing. Objects created using the Scissors tool will retain the per-object parameters of the object from which they were cut.

Figure 2.21

THE ARROW TOOL

The Arrow tool serves the following multiple editing functions:

» **Selection.** Click in the middle of a Correction object to select it for editing, or select multiple Correction objects by clicking-and-dragging horizontally inside the Pitch Graph display.

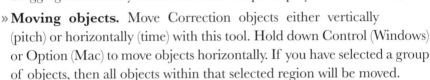

Figure 2.22

» **Moving objects.** Move Correction objects either vertically (pitch) or horizontally (time) with this tool. Hold down Control (Windows) or Option (Mac) to move objects horizontally. If you have selected a group of objects, then all objects within that selected region will be moved.

» **Editing the length of Correction objects.** Click on a Line or Curve object's end point to move that point vertically or horizontally (again, you must use the above mentioned key modifiers for horizontal movements). For Line objects that can contain anchor points within the line itself, you can use the Arrow tool to click on those anchor points (or between them) to edit the segment's shape and placement. Click on the edge of a Note object and drag to extend or shorten it (as shown in the Note object walk-through).

» **Adding or deleting anchor points.** Double-clicking with the Arrow tool on a portion of a Line object will add an anchor point at the click point, which can then be moved as described above. Double-clicking on top of an existing anchor point will delete it from the Line object.

3 ANTARES AUTO-TUNE EFX 2

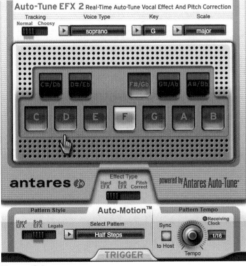

Figure 3.1

Antares Audio Technologies' Auto-Tune EFX series of pitch correction plugins balances ease of use with professional pitch correction, both as a tool and as an effect.

Auto-Tune EFX 2 does not have an offline mode editing environment. It works during playback or tracking in your DAW or when live audio routed to your DAW is sent through it.

AUTO-TUNE EFX 2 DETAILS

» **Format: AU, VST, RTAS**

» **License System: iLok**

» **Price: $129**

AUTO-TUNE EFX 2 PARAMETERS IN FOCUS

The primary difference between Auto-Tune EFX 2 and its predecessor, EFX 1, is Auto-Motion, a customizable pattern-generating feature that can add melody and zing to a vocal part. Auto-Tune EFX 2's pitch correction features and its Auto-Motion features are largely independent of one another, and therefore are covered here separately.

AUTO-TUNE EFX 2 PITCH CORRECTION PARAMETERS

Let's look at Auto-Tune EFX 2's pitch parameters first. Some of these will look familiar, because they are similar to other versions of Auto-Tune and other pitch correction titles examined in this book.

» **Tracking.** This setting helps dial in the pitch detection process. Auto-Tune EFX 2 incorporates this setting on a switch with two settings—Normal and Choosy. Normal works ideally in most cases.

» **Input Type.** This setting helps Auto-Tune focus its pitch detection within a defined boundary of frequencies. The following choices are available: Soprano, Alto/Tenor, Baritone/Bass, and Instrument (for nonvocal monophonic material). When in doubt, try Alto/Tenor.

» **Key.** This drop-down menu offers the expected keys from A to G available in half steps.

» **Scale.** The choices here are Major, Minor, and Chromatic.

» **Effect Type.** This three-way switch offers two types of the Auto-Tune effect, labeled Hard EFX and Soft EFX. They determine how pronounced the effect will be. The third setting, Pitch Correct, offers typical pitch correction as a tool and not as an effect. This is the only way to adjust the all-important Retune Speed parameter in this plug-in.

» **Note buttons.** Front and center in the Auto-Tune EFX 2 display are its Note buttons, which cover all notes in half steps. When these buttons are colored blue, they are included in the current scale and correction will be applied based on them. When they are black or white, they are removed from the scale, and therefore pitch correction will be applied based on the next closest note.

Figure 3.2

AUTO-TUNE EFX 2'S AUTO-MOTION PARAMETERS

As described above, Auto-Tune EFX 2's Auto-Motion feature allows you to add or augment the melody of the audio being processed by Auto-Tune. The plug-in ships with a large selection of pattern choices that range from musical to special effects. Patterns can also be created or edited using the open source MusicXML notation file format. Such editing is beyond the scope of this book; however, Antares offers a document on the subject in the Auto-Tune EFX 2 program folder.

Here's a look at Auto-Tune EFX 2's Auto-Motion parameters.

» **Pattern Style.** This switch pertains only to Auto-Motion patterns. Hard EFX and Soft EFX settings work the same as their Effect Type counterparts described above. Legato offers a smooth transition between notes found in the Auto-Motion pattern.

This switch offers independent control between the effect setting for pitch correcting the overall track, and the type of correction employed on an Auto-Motion pattern. For example, setting Pitch Correct for the Effect Type and Hard EFX for the Pattern Style means the Auto-Tune effect will occur on the track only when Auto-Motion patterns are applied via the Trigger button.

Figure 3.3

» **Selected Pattern.** Clicking on the right-pointing arrow or the current pattern name under the Selected Pattern window opens a menu displaying the different Auto-Motion patterns available in Auto-Tune EFX 2.

» **Sync to Host.** Located under Auto-Motion's Pattern Tempo section, when selected, Sync to Host syncs Auto-Motion patterns to the tempo of your project. For this to happen, your DAW must send valid project clock information to its plug-ins. Most do, and Auto-Tune EFX 2's Receiving Clock will light up when this button is selected and clock data is being received.

» **Tempo.** When Sync to Host is selected, this knob establishes the divisor or multiplier of the project clock's beat values, from whole notes to 32nd-note triplets. When Sync to Host is not selected, the Tempo knob's value changes to a beat per minute control, ranging from 20 to 260.

» **Trigger.** To engage a pattern during playback, click-and-hold the Auto-Motion Trigger button located at the bottom of the plug-in window. This control can be automated so that when you are rendering the plug-in's processing or mixing down the project, the Auto-Motion patterns are played at the proper time.

AUTO-TUNE EFX 2 IN ACTION

Here's a simple and effective walk-through that shows how to get the most out of this plug-in. It should be clear by now that all versions of Auto-Tune work with monophonic material only.

FAST TRACK TO THE AUTO-TUNE EFFECT

Since Auto-Tune EFX 2 lends itself quite well to achieving the popular Auto-Tune/Cher/T-Pain/Black Eyed Peas effect, the goal of this walk-through is to achieve this effect in as few steps as possible.

1. Place Auto-Tune EFX 2 as an insert on the audio track you wish to process with Auto-Tune.

2. Select the Key and Scale parameters if you know them. If not, set the Scale parameter to Chromatic.

3. Input Type should be set to match the singer's range. If you are unsure what to do here, leave it at its default setting of Alto/Tenor. Leave the Tracking switch set to Normal.

4. Set the Effect Type switch to Hard EFX.

5. Press Play on your DAW.

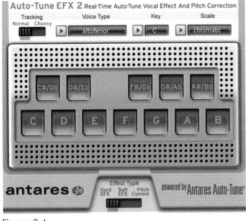

Figure 3.4

It's that simple. To help understand the pitch correction options available in this plug-in, try different Effect Type settings, and also deselect some of the notes in the selected scale to hear how removing them affects melody and the pitch correction process.

USING AUTO-TUNE EFX 2: WHEN YOU DO NOT KNOW THE SCALE OR KEY OF THE SONG

When the song's key and scale are unknown, or when it uses notes (accidentals) outside its primary scale and key), set Scale to chromatic, play back your track, and watch Auto-Tune EFX 2 while listening to the music, focusing on the vocal. Auto-Tune EFX 2 displays what notes it's correcting to via a small hand icon flashing near the note's button. Use this information along with your ears to deselect notes that do not belong with the part. It should be easy to dial in the right set of notes after a few listens and some trial and error. Turning these notes on and off via automation during certain parts of the song also goes a long way in dialing in pitch correction and augmenting melody.

Save this custom scale as an Auto-Tune preset using the Preset dialog box of your DAW's plug-in. Be sure to save your project as well.

Remember, when working with the Auto-Tune effect, the wider the interval between the original note and pitch-corrected note, the more pronounced the effect will be. Something to keep in mind when tracking your project as well as mixing.

4 IZOTOPE'S THE T-PAIN EFFECT:
PITCH CORRECTION WITH ATTITUDE

Figure 4.1

Don't let the highly stylized look of iZotope's The T-Pain Effect fool you—it is a serious piece of software for pitch correction and the T-Pain-style vocal effect. The T-Pain Effect plug-in is available separately or bundled with The T-Pain Engine and the T-Pain iDrum drum machine software. The T-Pain Engine standalone program is also available separately. This chapter focuses on vocal processing found in both The T-Pain Engine and The T-Pain Effect.

Figure 4.2

THE T-PAIN EFFECT DETAILS

» Format: AU, VST, RTAS, MAS, Direct X

» License System: iLok or System

» Price: $29 (The T-Pain Engine), $79 (The T-Pain Effect Plug-in only), $99 (The T-Pain Effect Bundle)

THE T-PAIN ENGINE

This standalone version of The T-Pain Effect is designed for creating fully realized songs, primarily but not exclusively within the hip-hop and rap genres. Users can record (or import) two vocal tracks and lay them against any of the dozens of T-Pain-approved beats and grooves included with the software. Each vocal can get its own T-Pain Effect or standard pitch correction treatment. Beats are broken down into 15 different sections including turnarounds, choruses, verses, and intros. These four-beat segments appear as color coded segments on the beat track, and they can be easily rearranged using drop-down menus accessible from each segment. Creating custom beats this way is easy and intuitive, and the combinations are nearly endless. Finished songs can be exported as .wav files or uploaded directly from the program to SoundCloud. The software offers an optional Sound Check dialog box to help audio production newbies get up and running quickly. To change setup or tweak how

The T-Pain Engine is connected to audio hardware and software, users can revisit Sound Check at any time by clicking on its button on the left-hand side of the display.

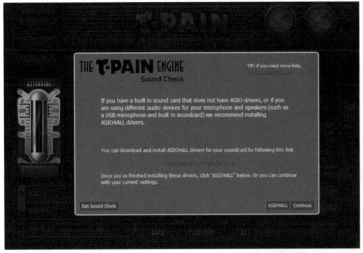

Figure 4.3

THE T-PAIN ENGINE VOCAL TRACKS

Vocal tracks can receive pitch correction processing in real time without being recorded into the program. This makes the program a great solution for live applications requiring standard pitch correction and pitch correction effects.

Clicking on the FX button on the right-hand side of The T-Pain Engine opens a set of controls that mirror the plug-in version of The T-Pain Effect. In addition, three types of reverb can be independently applied to each of the two vocal tracks.

Figure 4.4

THE T-PAIN EFFECT PLUG-IN

The plug-in version of The T-Pain Effect streamlines the pitch correction process, and is ideal when the ubiquitous vocal effect is the goal. Its transparent pitch correction processing is nothing to sneeze at. Unlike the standalone version, it belongs as an audio insert on the vocal track in need of pitch correction.

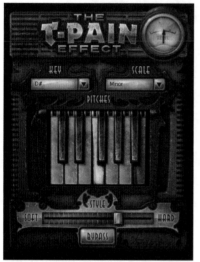

Figure 4.5

ACHIEVING THE T-PAIN EFFECT WITH THE T-PAIN EFFECT

Here are a few steps to help you quickly achieve both the T-Pain sound and transparent pitch correction. While this walk-through focuses on The T-Pain Effect plug-in, it also applies to the FX portion of the standalone T-Pain Engine.

1. Open The T-Pain Effect as an audio insert on the track to which you wish to apply pitch correction.

2. Set The T-Pain Effect's Scale and Key for your song and vocal part. If you do not know the best scale and key for the song, select Chromatic and read on.

3. Set the level of desired effect using the Style slider at the bottom of the plug-in window. Move the slider all the way to the left for transparent vocal correction. Moving it right delivers various degrees of the well-known effect.

4. Play back the audio. While listening to the effect on the vocal against the music track, watch the piano keys in the plug-in window. They will light up, showing you which notes the plug-in is pitch-correcting to. When the Scale parameter is set to Chromatic, pitch correction is applied to the closest semitone and therefore may not sound pronounced, and vibrato passages may get corrected to multiple notes. Watch the keys to see which light up the most frequently. Dial in the scale by turning off surrounding keys (clicking on them turns keys on or off). This conforms pitch correction to the notes that the plug-in finds most frequently in the vocal track. Turning on and off different notes while playing the track over and over is a quick way to find the best scale for the vocal part being affected, and to help define a melody for the vocal.

The T-Pain Effect's piano keys will be darker in color when they are used in the scale, and lighter in color when not used. They always light up during playback to show you which notes are part of the pitch correction process.

You can also experiment by choosing different Key and Scale settings from their respective drop-down menus. With only four scale settings not counting Chromatic (major, minor, major pentatonic, minor pentatonic), and the typical 12 keys (A through G♯ in half steps or semitones), dialing in these values during playback is fast and easy.

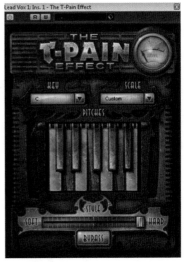

Figure 4.6

THE T-PAIN EFFECT AS A PITCH CORRECTION TOOL

While The T-Pain Effect will be at home in production environments where the vocal effect is predominately used, it also is well suited for situations in which pitch correction needs are basic. Lite versions of advanced technologies such as pitch correction are not only affordable, but they also expedite workflow by surfacing just the fundamental parameters required to get the job done. For example, on vocal tracks that just need a bit of caressing in order to meet today's in-tune requirements, setting The T-Pain Effect's Scale to Chromatic and spending a minute to find the sweet spot on the Style slider can achieve excellent results quickly.

5 IZOTOPE NECTAR:
THE NEW AGE OF PITCH CORRECTION AND VOCAL PROCESSING

Figure 5.1

Nectar is, using iZotope's language, a "Complete Vocal Suite." Within its attractive GUI, users will find preamp and saturation emulation; de-essers; maximizers; compressors; EQ; effects such as reverb, doubling, and echo; and, of course, pitch correction, which we'll focus on here. There are 11 different processing modules in all. How you access them depends on workflow considerations that Nectar manages through its Genre and Style Selector.

NECTAR DETAILS

» **Format: AU, VST, RTAS, MAS, Direct X**

» **License System: iLok or System-based**

» **Price: $299**

THE NECTAR WORKFLOW

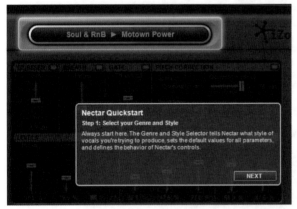

Figure 5.2

When launching Nectar for the first time, you'll be walked through its initial genre/style workflow methodology in a brief, quick-start tutorial that introduces users to the plug-in's core features. This tutorial is highly effective at getting users up to speed quickly without having to crack the manual. It helps that the program, in spite of its long list of features, is user-friendly.

THE GENRE AND STYLE SELECTOR

The first step in using Nectar is to select one of its 12 genres, and then one of the many styles available within that genre. This tells the program which modules to load and what default settings they will have. All this can be tweaked at the user's discretion. This is a great approach, especially when working in musical genres outside your comfort area.

Figure 5.3

Here's a list of Nectar's 12 genres. Each genre contains anywhere from 5 to 12 different styles.

» Alternative and Indie

» Classical

» Country

» Dance and Electronic

» Folk

» Hip-Hop and Rap

» Jazz

» Pop

» Rock

» Soul and R&B

» Special FX

» Voice Over and Dialog

New genres and styles can be added, and old ones can be removed. Default parameters and settings can likewise be edited for each style. This allows single-click loading of a personalized set of finely tuned modules tailored to your production needs and workflow.

NECTAR'S MAIN VIEW

Nectar's Main View contains three sets of vocal processing sections: Tools, Enhance, and EQ.

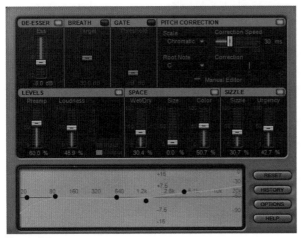

Figure 5.4

THE TOOLS SECTION

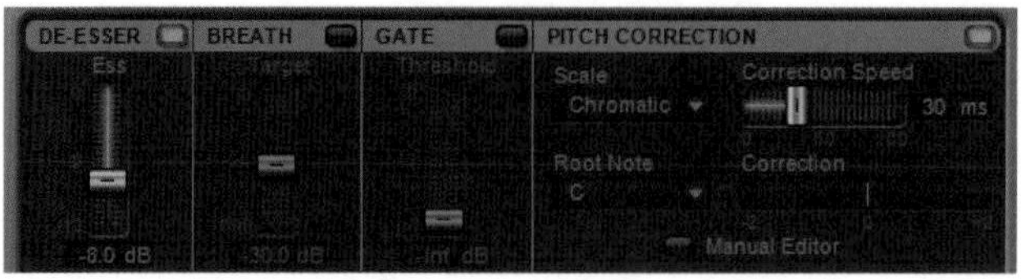

Figure 5.5

This section contains a de-esser, a breath reducer (unavailable in Tracking mode), a gate, and Nectar's automatic pitch correction module.

THE ENHANCE SECTION

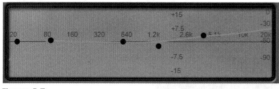

Figure 5.6

The Enhance section contains a Levels module with Preamp and Loudness sliders, a Space module that will contain various forms of echo or reverb, depending on the loaded genre and style; and a Creative module that is also unique to the selected genre and style.

THE EQUALIZER SECTION

Figure 5.7

This section contains an equalizer with five different nodes across the standard 20 Hz to 20 kHz frequency spectrum. Individual or groups of nodes can be moved horizontally across the frequency spectrum, and vertically to add or subtract gain at or around the node's frequency location.

Each node can have its own EQ type. This can be changed by right-clicking on the node, which opens a dialog box showing the seven different EQ types available—from parametric-style bell-shaped curves to high and low shelves and passes.

REAL-TIME (AUTOMATIC) PITCH CORRECTION IN NECTAR'S MAIN VIEW

Pitch correction in Nectar's Main View is real time and easy to use. Most of Nectar's genres and styles do not have pitch correction turned on, which is why it's a good idea to customize or create a new style with pitch correction engaged and its default settings established on your preferences. Turn this function on by clicking on the oval switch at the top right of the Pitch Correction module.

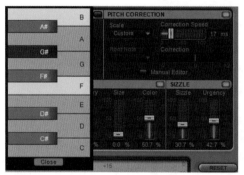

Figure 5.8

Nectar's Main View pitch correction reveals only three parameters, a meter showing how much correction is being applied, and, when the Custom scale setting is chosen, a piano roll used for creating that custom scale. More parameters are available in Advanced View described below; however, professional pitch correction can be dialed in with this minimal set.

To apply pitch correction from Nectar's Main View, simply set the Root Note, Scale, and Correction Speed parameters. Correction Speed controls how quickly pitch correction is applied. At settings ranging from 0 to 15 milliseconds (ms), expect the well-known vocal effect. At slower speeds, expect various levels of transparent pitch correction.

Nectar's Scale parameter offers four different scales: Major, Minor, Chromatic, and Custom. Clicking on Custom opens a window displaying a single-octave piano keyboard. Clicking on these keys turns them on or off, allowing you to create custom scales. Turned off keys cause pitches near that key to be corrected to the next-closest note.

While Nectar's real-time pitch correction will do the job in many instances, surgically precise offline pitch correction is available via the Manual Editor button in the Main View pitch correction module, or from the Advanced View pitch correction module.

ADVANCED VIEW CONTROLS FOR AUTOMATIC MODE PITCH CORRECTION

While the three parameters in Nectar's Main View pitch correction module may be all you ever need, Nectar's advanced automatic pitch correction parameters are there when things need a bit more tweaking.

Under Advanced View, additional parameters are available for each of Nectar's 11 modules. For pitch processing, these advanced controls include parameters for both automatic and manual pitch correction when Nectar is in Mixing mode, and automatic only when Nectar is in Tracking mode. Since Tracking mode is designed to use fewer system resources, it employs a streamlined pitch correction algorithm, and only automatic pitch correction is available.

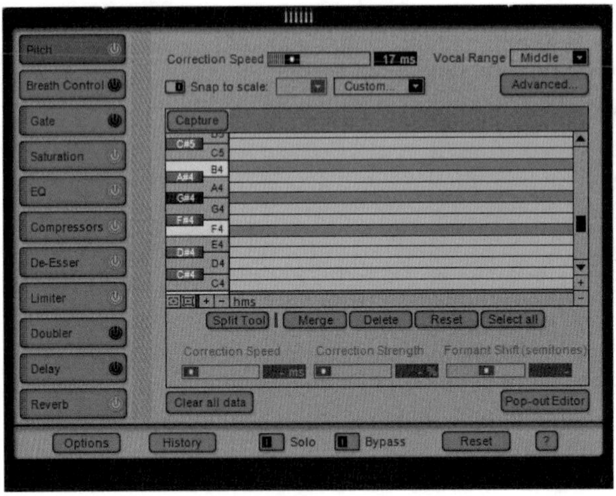

Figure 5.9

Here's a closer look at the additional pitch correction parameters available from Advanced View's Pitch module.

» **Correction Speed.** As discussed previously, this parameter controls how fast pitch correction is applied. At very fast speeds, you will be engaging pitch correction as an effect. Slower speeds allow for more natural and transparent pitch correction.

» **Vocal Range.** Use this parameter to specify the source audio's vocal range, which helps the pitch detection process. The choices here are Low, Middle, and High. Middle works great in most instances.

» **Snap to Scale.** This parameter is turned on by default, and causes Nectar pitch correction to snap to the notes established by the Scale and Root Note settings. Automatic pitch correction will not work if Snap to Scale is turned off.

» **Root Note and Scale.** These two parameters establish the notes to which the source audio will be pitch-corrected.

» **Piano Roll.** This option is available by choosing Custom in the Scale drop-down menu from either Main View or Advanced View. Click on keys to turn them on or off, thereby creating a custom pitch correction scale.

These next parameters are available by clicking on the Advanced button while in the Advanced Pitch Correction module or from the Manual Editor pop-out window.

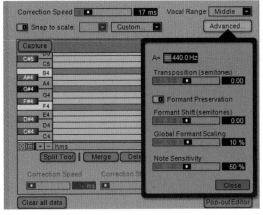

Figure 5.10

» **Reference Pitch.** If the audio you are pitch-correcting with Nectar used a reference pitch different than the default A4 = 440 Hz, then double-click and enter that value here, or use its virtual scroll wheel inside the display. Having the right setting here ensures that corrected notes will match the source audio's reference pitch. This parameter should always be set prior to audio capture. If audio is present in the pitch correction module when changing reference pitch, it will need to be cleared and recaptured.

» **Transpose.** This parameter allows you to transpose the source audio in semitones. The range is one octave below and above the original pitch.

» **Formant Preservation.** Enabled by default, this parameter preserves the all-important formant characteristics contained in the source vocal. Without it, large changes in pitch would not sound natural. When this parameter is turned on, two related parameters, Formant Shifting and Formant Scaling, become available.

» **Formant Shifting.** This control allows users to manually adjust vocal formant shifts in semitones. To get a feel for what this and the following Formant Scaling parameters do, adjust them during playback.

» **Formant Scaling.** This parameter helps formant preservation by allowing users to adjust the formant scale up or down in accordance with large changes in pitch. For example, if the pitch correction process moved notes up an entire octave, adjusting this parameter can help match the formants to that higher pitch. iZotope suggests setting Formant Scaling to maximum when working with pitch correction as an effect.

» **Note Sensitivity.** This parameter controls how sensitive Nectar will be in determining which notes require pitch correction. At lower settings, fewer notes in the source audio will be corrected, and at higher settings, more notes in the source audio will be corrected. Note Sensitivity is available only when Nectar is in Mixing mode.

Double-clicking on any automatic mode pitch correction parameter will return it to its default state.

MANUAL PITCH CORRECTION IN NECTAR

One of the themes in this book is that manual (graphical) mode pitch correction offers the highest degree of pitch editing precision. Nectar's manual pitch correction is no different, and its ease of use (a theme throughout the Nectar interface) makes it accessible to newbies and pros alike.

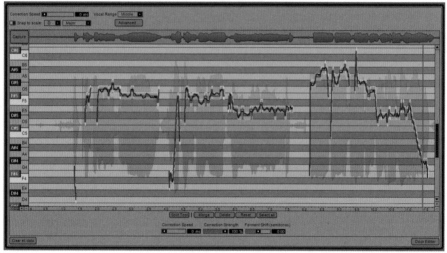

Figure 5.11

Since pitch editing takes place inside Nectar's Manual Editor display, it's important to understand how to navigate around this area.

» **Vertical Scroll.** Use the arrows and slider on the right side of the Manual Editor display to scroll the view of reference pitch bars and Note regions.

» **Vertical Zoom.** Use the plus or minus buttons beneath the vertical slider to zoom in vertically.

» **Horizontal Scroll.** Drag the light orange box resting over the macro view of the waveform (located to the right of the Capture button) to the left or right to view different portions of the waveform inside the Manual Editor display.

» **Horizontal Zoom.** Use the plus or minus zoom buttons located beneath the piano roll to zoom in or out horizontally. You can also click-and-drag the ends of the light orange box atop the macro view of the waveform to adjust how much of the tracked audio is visible.

» **Zoom Fit.** Click on the bracketed minus button (located to the left of the horizontal zoom buttons) to focus all captured note data (shown as Note regions) in the Manual Editor window.

» **Zoom to Selection.** Click on the bracketed plus button to focus in on selected Note regions.

CAPTURING AUDIO FOR NECTAR'S MANUAL PITCH CORRECTION

Manual pitch correction in Nectar is available only in Mixing mode, and like other offline or graphical modes, it requires capturing the audio before pitch correction can take place. Nectar's workflow invites users to establish settings for Root Note, Scale, and Correction Speed prior to audio capture. While this can speed up workflow, it is not a requirement since these settings can also be applied to the Note regions created during audio capture and used for pitch manipulation.

The following walk-through illustrates how easy it is to manually apply pitch correction in Nectar.

1. Nectar should be set to Mixing mode, with Main View as the current view. Turn on the pitch correction module if it is not already on, and set its Main View parameters for the track destined for pitch correction. (Remember, all pitch correction plug-ins should be opened as an audio insert.)

2. Click on the Manual Editor button from the Main View Pitch Correction module. This opens a large, separate window dedicated for manual, graphical-style pitch correction. (This same window is also available by clicking on the Pop-Out Editor button in Advanced View's Pitch Correction module.

   The Manual Editor window is where we will capture audio for our offline pitch editing. Grab the right corner of the Manual Editor window and drag it out so it fills a good portion of your screen. This gives you the most room to work with for manual pitch editing.

The parameters at the top of the Manual Editor window replicate the parameters at the top of the Advanced View Pitch Correction module.

3. Turn on Snap to Scale if it is not already on. When turned on prior to audio capture, Snap to Scale applies automatic pitch correction during the capture, and Main View pitch correction settings (also shown at the top of the Manual Editor window) are applied to the Note regions created during capture. If Snap to Scale is turned off, Nectar will detect the pitches of the captured audio, but correction will not be applied until you manually edit and move Note regions. Having Snap to Scale turned on during Capture is like importing Automatic mode pitch correction settings into the Manual Editor. This is a great workflow methodology, so let's leave it on for this walk-through. Later, you can move these Note regions as needed for fine-tuning pitch correction.

4. Click on the Capture button. It will light up and its text will change to "Capturing," showing it is ready to receive audio. Start playback of your DAW at the point where you wish to capture audio for pitch correction. Always start playback at a point where there is no audio on the track to avoid glitches in correction. During capture, a sample-accurate waveform representation will appear in the Manual Editor display, along with pitch correction Note regions based on the settings established by the Main View Pitch Correction module parameters.

Stop the DAW transport when capture is completed.

For reference, pitches are shown as horizontal bars across the captured waveform graphic. They start from the piano roll on the left-hand vertical axis of the Manual Editor display.

NOTE REGIONS AND PITCH CONTOURS

Note regions and their associated settings are what you manipulate for manual pitch correction processing. They are displayed as orange blocks resting over the waveform.

Two types of pitch contours (they look like wavy lines) are also created during audio capture. Original Pitch contours are black and they show the pitch curves detected by Nectar. Corrected Pitch contours are orange. They reflect the final output pitch based on Note region placement and settings. Orange Corrected Pitch contours can mask the black Original Pitch contours. This is okay since both of these contours are for reference only. When you click-and-drag Note regions to new pitches, any hidden Original Pitch contours will be revealed.

MANUAL PITCH EDITING IN NECTAR

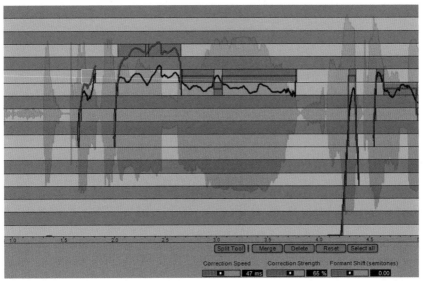

Figure 5.12

Surgical pitch correction is a breeze in Nectar's Manual Editor window. Simply click on a Note region and move it to the desired pitch. Reference pitches are played to aid you in placing them on the appropriate notes. It's quite simple. Try it. To move a Note region so it's not exactly on the note, hold down the Control (Windows) or Option (Mac) key when moving them. Groups of regions can be moved together if you first click-and-drag around a group of Note regions prior to moving.

Remember that if Snap to Scale was on during capture, Note regions are initially created based on the settings shown at the top of the Manual Editor window (these match the Main View settings). In such cases, pitch correction has already been applied, and may only need a bit of finessing. If Snap to Scale is off, then pitch correction begins with Note region moves and manipulations.

PITCH CORRECTION SETTINGS PER NOTE REGION

A cornerstone to manual pitch editing is having the ability to assign different correction parameters to each Note region. This is key to highly professional and transparent pitch correction results. It also gives supreme control over the application of pitch correction as an effect.

Edit the correction parameters of any selected Note region (or groups of regions) via the controls beneath the Manual Editor display. Notice a new parameter here—Correction Strength. This control serves to humanize the pitch correction process. At higher Correction Strength values, the pitch is corrected to the specified note to a greater degree (something you would want when using pitch correction as an effect). For example with a Correction Strength of 100%, the entire Note region is corrected to the specified pitch. At lower Correction Strength values, the nuances of the part being corrected are better preserved.

Experiment with Correction Speed and Correction Strength sliders while watching the Corrected Pitch contour of the currently selected Note region. This provides insight into how these two important parameters work together to edit and manipulate pitch.

USING CORRECTION SPEED AND AMOUNT PARAMETERS TO ADJUST CORRECTION CONTOURS

The following guidelines will help you use Pitch contours for reference while using Correction Speed and Correction Amount Settings for transparent pitch correction and pitch correction effects. Remember that these controls work on Note regions that can be selected individually, in groups, or across the entire track.

» **Transparent pitch correction.** The wider the Original Pitch contour shape, the greater the variance in pitch, and, most likely, the greater the need for pitch correction. Start with a Correction Speed of around 30 ms, dial up Correction Amount to tame (narrow) the Corrected Pitch contour and thus better control unintended or poorly performed pitch modulations. Listen as the contour narrows to find the sweet spot between these controls. The right level of correction will be heard as an in-tune performance that does not sound processed or robotic. For highly transparent pitch correction, Corrected Pitch contours should resemble the Original Pitch contours, though the width of the corrected contour should be diminished—reflecting a more in-tune performance. The overall Corrected Pitch contour should also be centered on the correct note based on Note region placement.

» **Quantized pitch effects.** For T-Pain-style pitch effects, correction contours should flatten out dramatically, even as far as becoming straight lines. Accomplish this by first setting the Correction Speed to zero, and the correction amount to 100%. When going for vocal effects, be sure to also set Global Formant Scaling to its maximum 40%.

MANUAL PITCH EDITING TOOLS

Figure 5.13

Nectar's manual pitch editor also offers several tools for editing Note regions. Buttons for these tools are located beneath the Manual Editor display.

» **Split Tool.** Click on this tool, and then click on a Note region to split it at the click point. This tool turns itself off after every click unless you hold down the Shift key while using it. Cutting large Note regions into smaller ones allows for more precise pitch processing. Moving these smaller Note regions to different pitches gives more control over effect-driven melody editing.

» **Merge.** To merge any cut Note regions or adjacent Note regions, select them and then click on the Merge button.

» **Delete.** Clicking on this button deletes any selected regions. It's a good idea to remove Note regions wherever pitch correction is not required.

» **Reset.** Clicking on this button resets the selected Note region back to its original location (assuming that it had been moved). You can also double-click on a Note region to do this.

» **Select All.** This button selects all Note regions, which can then be moved or have their settings changed.

» **Clear All Data.** This button at the bottom right of the Manual Editor window clears all captured audio and associated pitch correction data.

» **Dock Editor.** Click on this button to close the Pop-Out editor. You can also click on the Manual Editor's red "x" at the top right corner of its window.

6 WAVES TUNE: PRO PITCH CORRECTION FROM A PLUG-IN POWERHOUSE

Waves is well known for making excellent, great-sounding, professional plug-ins. The company's pitch correction plug-in Waves Tune is no exception and offers the same kind of comprehensive feature set that Waves plug-ins are known for.

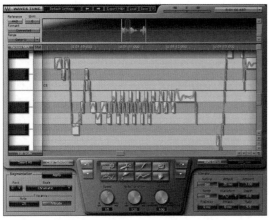

Figure 6.1

WAVES TUNE DETAILS

» **Format: AU, VST, RTAS**

» **License System: Proprietary. System-based or flash drive licensing.**

» **Price: $400 ($79 for the lite version)**

WAVES TUNE INS AND OUTS

Waves Tune pitch correction is an offline process only. That is, audio must be scanned into the plug-in before any pitch correction processing can occur. Waves Tune uses the ReWire software protocol for transferring audio from your DAW and to sync the plug-in with your DAW's transport and session time. This ReWire connection happens automatically unless you are using Pro Tools, which requires creating a ReWire plug-in instance prior to launching Waves Tune. Using ReWire allows the DAW's transport control to work simultaneously for both the project and the plug-in while maintaining perfect sync.

When scanning audio into Waves Tune, several elements appear inside the plug-in.

» **Waveform Overview.** Located above the Pitch Edit Graph, it shows the entire tracked waveform, along with project markers and time cursor position. A rectangle overlay appears over the waveform here denoting the portion currently visible in the Pitch Edit Graph. Click-and-drag this rectangle horizontally to display different parts of the waveform inside the Pitch Edit Graph.

» **Detected Pitch curve.** Detected pitches of the scanned audio are shown as a series of orange curves inside the Pitch Edit Graph. Depending on how far out of tune the source audio is, and the current pitch correction settings, these orange curves may be masked by Correction Pitch curves.

» **Correction Pitch curve.** Corrected pitches are shown as green curves in the Pitch Edit Graph. During audio scanning, these green curves (along with the Note segments described below) are created based on the Root and Scale settings found in the Segmentation section located at the bottom left of the plug-in window. These and other pitch correction parameters can be easily changed at any time.

» **Note Segments.** These square or rectangle blocks in the Pitch Edit Graph can be moved individually or in groups to different pitches as needed. They can also receive specific pitch correction parameters for fine-tuning your pitch correction work.

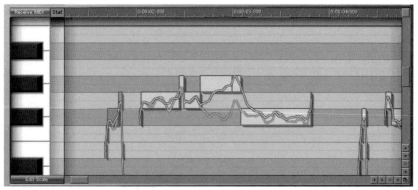

Figure 6.2

THE PITCH EDIT GRAPH

The Pitch Edit Graph is Waves Tune's pitch editing and pitch reference environment. It fills up much of the plug-in's display and resembles similar graphical environments found in other plug-ins covered in this book. Pitch is referenced by a piano roll on the vertical axis. A correction grid stems from this axis consisting of bars representing pitches defined by that piano roll. Note segments on this grid can be moved to different pitch locations defined by this grid.

Time is referenced on the horizontal axis. Typical scrollbars and plus and minus zoom buttons are available for navigation and viewing purposes.

WAVES TUNE'S GLOBAL PARAMETERS

The following global parameters should be set prior to scanning audio. Changes to these parameters after scanning requires a new audio scan.

» **Reference Pitch.** The default is A4 = 440 Hz. If the project's audio used a different reference pitch, set that value here prior to scanning audio. Changing this setting after scanning requires a rescan of audio intoWaves Tune.

» **Range.** This parameter focuses Waves Tune's pitch detection to specific ranges, which can aid the pitch detection process. The choices are Generic, Bass, Baritone, Tenor, Alto, Mezzo Soprano, and Soprano. Generic is ideal for parts that cover more than one range. The Pitch Edit Graph will gray out pitches excluded by this setting.

The following global parameters can be set at any time without negatively impacting workflow.

» **Global Pitch Shift.** This shifts the pitch of all scanned audio. The range is plus or minus 12 equal-tempered semitones. Values are in cents (100 cents = 1 semitone or half step).

» **Formant Correction.** This setting turns on or off formant correction for the scanned audio. This should be left on in most instances, especially if pitch correction shifts notes a semitone or more. Try turning it off when using Waves Tune to correct nonvocal parts.

WAVES TUNE'S SEGMENTATION SECTION: DIALING IN PITCH CORRECTION PRIOR TO SCANNING

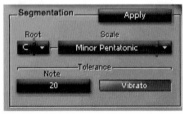

Waves Tune applies pitch correction to the scanned audio based on the settings found in the Segmentation section. Let's look at the parameters found here:

Figure 6.3

» **Root.** Set the root note for the selected scale with this menu. Choices are A through G♯ in half steps. Setting this parameter (along with the Scale parameter) prior to scanning audio improves workflow by placing Note segments based on these settings. Both Root and Scale can be changed at any time.

» **Scale.** This parameter sets the scale to which pitch correction will be applied. The default is Chromatic. Waves Tune offers a whopping 43 different scales including blues, bebop, and major and minor pentatonic. This setting defines the status of notes shown in the Pitch Edit Graph's correction grid. Legal notes fall within the scale; illegal notes fall outside of the scale, though they can still contain Note segments.

» **Tolerance Control.** Use this parameter to help manage the creation of Note segments. At higher settings it can ignore small changes in pitch and thus create fewer Note segments. At lower settings, those same changes in pitch may end up receiving Note segments. This parameter can be set before or after scanning audio, and can be changed at any time. The default setting works great most of the time.

» **Vibrato Segmentation.** Located under the Tolerance subsection, this parameter helps prevent Waves Tune from creating Note segments across different pitches detected in an existing vibrato. When turned on, Waves Tune creates Note segments based on the average pitch found within that vibrato. A red highlight will appear over Note segments wherever this has been applied. This parameter should be applied after scanning audio.

WAVES TUNE'S ONE-STEP AUDIO SCANNING

Scanning audio into Waves Tune is quite easy. Set the global parameters as needed, define the correct pitches using the Root and Scale parameters, and then start playback using your DAW's transport controls. Stop when you've captured the audio you wish to pitch-correct. With Waves Tune you need only scan in the portion of audio in need of correction, and you can scan additional parts of the same track at any time without losing sync. Waves Tune can accept up to ten minutes of audio.

Depending on production goals, the project's pitch requirements, and Waves Tune's Segmentation settings, it is possible that pitch correction has been sufficiently processed upon completion of audio scanning. Play back the track using your DAW's transport—both with the track soloed, and against the music to hear what, if any, additional pitch editing is required.

When additional pitch work is required, you will be primarily working with those blocky Note segments located inside the Pitch Edit Graph. Use Waves Tune's sliders, zoom buttons, and Zoom (represented by a magnifying glass icon) and Navigation (represented by a hand icon) tools located beneath the Pitch Edit Graph in the Graphic Tools section to focus in on the Note segments you wish to work with.

THE CORRECTION PARAMETERS SECTION

Note segments created by Waves Tune contain default values for Speed, Note Transitions, and Ratio. Let's take a look at what these critical pitch correction parameters do. Knobs for these parameters are located beneath the Waves Tune's Tools section.

Figure 6.4

» **Speed.** The speed at which correction is applied is a key contributor to pitch correction as an effect and as a transparent processing tool. This knob sets how long in milliseconds a note must be out of tune before correction is applied. At 0 ms, the well-known Cher/T-Pain effect is achieved. At settings of 15 ms (the default) and higher, Waves Tune delivers various levels of transparent pitch correction.

» **Note Transition.** This parameter sets a correction speed for transitions between different pitches. At fast values, this parameter helps achieve pitch correction effects. At slower values, it helps preserve pitch correction transparency between different notes. The default setting is 120 ms.

» **Ratio.** This option defines how much of the correction curve, the shape of which is largely defined by Speed and Note Transition settings, gets applied to the scanned audio. This serves to "humanize" pitch correction processing.

USING THE CORRECTION PARAMETERS SECTION FOR BOTH TRANSPARENT PITCH CORRECTION AND EFFECT PURPOSES

Waves Tune's Correction parameters (Speed, Note Transition, and Ratio) can be applied to a single Note segment or groups of Note segments, or the entire track via the Select All button. Here are some tips on applying these powerful parameters:

» For maximum pitch correction transparency between large shifts in pitch, use slower Note Transition settings across Note segments where transitions occur.

» Use faster Note Transition settings (try zero) to emphasize a vocal effect.

» Setting Speed and Note Transition to their fastest settings and Ratio to 100% delivers fantastic pitch correction effect results.

» Tweak correction parameters on a per-object basis to help manage effect levels and help emphasize the vocal effect on specific passages, such as a chorus.

» Decrease Ratio settings on segments where nuances key to the performance should come through without any (or with minimal) pitch correction.

» Apply slower correction speeds and lower ratios on segments where vibrato is present and should be preserved.

All in all, this is a highly intuitive process and mastering this section of Waves Tune is key to mastering all forms of pitch correction. Let your ears be your guide.

A TOUR OF WAVES TUNE'S GRAPHIC EDITING TOOLS

It should be clear by now that Waves Tune's workflow is geared around manipulating Note segments and editing their correction values. Waves makes doing both things intuitive and easy, while maintaining highly professional results. Much of this is accomplished using Waves Tune's Graphic Editing tools located just below the Pitch Edit Graph. They are also available by right-clicking anywhere inside the main Pitch Edit Graph area.

Figure 6.5

> » **The Note tool.** Use this tool to select Note segments (click on them) or groups of Note segments (click on and draw around a group of segments or Shift-click on multiple segments). Once selected, you can use this tool to move them to different pitches, or change their start or end points (simply move the cursor to a Note segment boundary, then click-and-drag). Selected Note segments can be assigned their own unique Speed, Note Transition, and Ratio values. You can also assign Vibrato Tolerance to selected Note segments to help Waves Tune ignore existing vibrato settings, or assign vibrato creation settings from Waves Tune's Vibrato section.

> » **The Slice tool.** Use this tool to cut a Note segment into two or more parts, which can then be edited or dragged to different pitches. This helps keep pitch editing surgically precise, and also aids in melody manipulation when working with pitch correction as an effect.

> » **The Pencil tool.** This tool allows you to draw your own pitch correction curves, which replaces Correction Pitch curve data existing in the same time location.

> » **The Zoom tool.** Displayed as a magnifying glass icon, click-and-drag with this tool to create a section that will be zoomed and focused inside the Pitch Edit Graph. Clicking inside the Pitch Edit Graph will zoom in one step. Click while holding down the Alt key to zoom out one step.

> » **The Curve tool.** Use this tool to move a pitch correction curve up or down to different pitches. Click on the beginning or ends of correction curves to create diagonal shifts in the curve. This tool is quite useful for adding or taming pitch glides.

> » **The Glue tool.** This tool "glues" multiple Note segments together into a single segment. When connecting segments located at different pitches, this tool always uses the pitch of the left-most Note segment.

» **The Line tool.** This tool is similar to the Pencil tool, only instead of drawing curves it draws straight lines. Single-click during the line-drawing process to create segment points within the line, and double-click to stop drawing the line. Lines can be drawn at angles across different pitches. This tool can also be put to excellent use when working with pitch correction as an effect and for melody re-creation.

» **Navigation tool.** This "handy" tool (exemplified by a hand icon) can be used to move what is visible around the Pitch Edit Graph.

CUSTOMIZING SCALES IN WAVES TUNE

Waves Tune offers some slick scale customizations inside the Pitch Edit Graph. Choose almost any scale from the Segmentation section, and notice that notes in the Pitch Edit Graph that are not part of the selected scale (also defined by the Root parameter) are marked as illegal in the Note Status column. When tracking in audio while illegal notes have been defined, the source audio close to an illegal note will be corrected to the next closest note. For example, if root and scale are set to G major prior to tracking, and the source audio contains a note closest to F, which is not part of a G major scale, then that note will be corrected to F♯ if it is sharp of F, or E if it is flat of F.

Click on any illegal note icon, and notice what happens—an upward pointing arrow replaces the illegal note icon. This indicates that pitches closest to the illegal note will be corrected to the next legal note above the illegal one you just clicked. Click on that icon again and a downward pointing arrow now appears, meaning that the note closest to this illegal note will be corrected to the next legal note lower in pitch. Click on that illegal note one more time and an *x* appears. This means that the note is bypassed entirely from the scale. Notes closest to a bypassed note will pass through unprocessed.

All the above scale-editing features can also apply to legal notes. Simply click on them in the Note Status column (the same column where the illegal note icon is located), just as you did for the illegal ones.

This is a great way to tailor scales to the performance and the song.

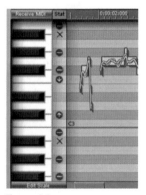

Figure 6.6

USING WAVES TUNE FOR THE EVER-POPULAR VOCAL EFFECT

Antares calls it the Auto-Tune Effect, T-Pain and iZotope call it the T-Pain Effect, the world calls it everything from the Cher effect (her hit "Believe" was the first time it was heard in popular music) to that "mechanical singing-robot sound you hear on the radio all the time." No matter what you call it, all the plug-ins covered in this book can deliver this ubiquitous effect. Here's how to get it in Waves Tune.

For all Note segments (or the ones that you want to contain the effect), set Speed and Note Transition to 0, and Ratio to 100%. That's it—you're done...well almost.

It bears repeating that when working with pitch correction as an effect, the greater the difference between detected pitch and corrected pitch, the more dramatic the effect will be. A simple way to strengthen the sound of pitch correction effects is to use the Note tool to move Note segments to notes far from the original pitch. Of course, make sure that Formant Correction is on.

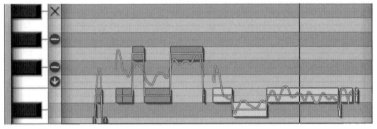

Figure 6.7

MIDI IN AND OUT OF WAVES TUNE

Scale and melody customization can be easily achieved via MIDI into Waves Tune. Each instance of the plug-in creates its own MIDI port that can receive MIDI data from any MIDI device or MIDI track mapped to it. To engage this feature, simply click on the Receive MIDI button above the piano roll. MIDI data must be received into the plug-in during scanning. That MIDI data overrides Waves Tune's Note segment creation as long as the data is present. When MIDI data is no longer present during a scan, Waves Tune reverts to using its Segmentation settings for segment creation.

Figure 6.8

MIDI into Waves Tune is a very powerful way to work with melody and to customize scales. And it's quite easy to do.

Waves Tune can also export its pitch correction data as a MIDI file that can be played by any MIDI device. Simply click on the Export MIDI button located at the top of the Waves Tune window. Note segments in the Pitch Edit Graph are exported as MIDI notes.

Exporting MIDI from Waves Tune is a great way for vocalists who do not have music theory training to write and create keyboard parts, melodies for the band, and even solos.

7 GRAMMY AWARD–WINNING PITCH CORRECTION WITH CELEMONY MELODYNE

Melodyne, by Grammy Award–winning Celemony Software, does a lot more than pitch correction, and is considered by many to be an indispensible production tool. It includes something that many believed impossible—polyphonic pitch correction via its DNA (Direct Note Access) technology.

Melodyne offers four different flavors of its pitch and time editing, from the lite version Melodyne Essential to the flagship Melodyne Editor, looked at here. Only Melodyne Editor includes DNA polyphonic pitch correction.

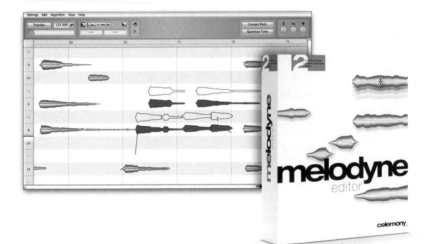

Figure 7.1

MELODYNE EDITOR DETAILS

» **Format: Standalone, ReWire, AU, VST, RTAS**

» **License System: System-based or iLok**

» **Price: $399**

THE MELODYNE PARADIGM

When first launched, Melodyne is essentially an empty window with surprisingly few menus and controls. But right-click almost anywhere inside the Melodyne window, and what you need is there where you need it. While the uber-clean user interface may startle some at first, Melodyne's revolutionary GUI is highly intuitive.

Both standalone and plug-in versions include Melodyne's toolbox menu, which offers comprehensive controls for time and pitch editing. Beneath this is the Inspector area, where you can enter values and scroll through them. On the far right of the Melodyne window are macro controls for pitch and time. The standalone version also contains a transport section for recording audio.

Figure 7.2

STANDALONE OR PLUG-IN?

Melodyne can operate as a standard audio plug-in inserted on the audio track in need of pitch or time correction. It can also be used standalone, similar to a wave editor. Via a ReWire connection, the standalone version of Melodyne can be synced to your DAW. For this type of workflow, simply launch your DAW and load your project before launching the standalone version of Melodyne. At launch, Melodyne will recognize the presence of your DAW and initiate a ReWire connection. Simply follow the prompts from there, and you should be good to go.

Each of these Melodyne operational modes is fully featured. For standalone instances of the software, you must load the audio file into the software, or record it directly from your audio interface. Typical audio interface setup options are available from the Preferences dialog box under Melodyne's File menu.

For the plug-in version, audio is transferred (recorded) in real time into the plug-in. Melodyne requires an audio buffer large enough to accommodate its sophisticated processing. At launch, the plug-in will warn you if the current buffer (latency) settings are inadequate.

MELODYNE STANDALONE WORKFLOW

Choosing how you launch Melodyne (inside or outside your DAW) is largely subjective and based on personal workflow preferences. The feature set is identical in both plug-in and standalone instances. If system resources are an issue, try exporting the audio track from your DAW and then open that file in the standalone version of Melodyne with no other applications running. Since vocal tracks are usually compiled from numerous takes, this is a great way to work when the project requires intensive Melodyne editing.

When you've finished editing in standalone mode, simply choose the Save As dialog box from the File menu, select the appropriate file format (usually .wav, although .aiff is also supported). The original audio format is preserved, with "orig" added to its name; this keeps your Melodyne work nondestructive.

EXPORTING MIDI FROM MELODYNE

In the standalone version, MIDI file export is handled in the same dialog box used for saving Melodyne edited audio. Just choose .mid as the file type. In the plug-in version, MIDI export is available from the Settings dialog box. Since Melodyne supports both monophonic and polyphonic material, guitar chord progressions and lead vocal melodies can both easily be exported as a MIDI file that can be played by virtually any MIDI device.

Melodyne's .mid files convert its pitches to MIDI notes, and MIDI note length and MIDI amplitude (volume) from the audio equivalents.

When saving as a .mid file, you have the option to create a MIDI file based solely on data between cycle points (equivalent to loop points) established inside Melodyne.

TRANSFERRING AUDIO INTO THE MELODYNE PLUG-IN

Melodyne is an offline, graphical pitch correction tool. As such, audio must be tracked into Melodyne for it to do its job. When launching the software as an audio insert on the track destined for Melodyne editing, the software's Transfer button flashes as a friendly reminder. Click on that button (it will turn a solid color), and then use your DAW's transport controls to play (transfer) the audio into Melodyne. Always start at a point prior to the presence of the audio data you wish to work with. Stop the transport when finished.

The remainder of this chapter assumes that you have transferred monophonic audio into Melodyne and are ready for pitch correction. Many of the monophonic pitch correction techniques also apply to polyphonic audio, so it's a good place to start. Working with polyphonic material is covered at the end of this chapter.

Upon completion of audio transfer, Melodyne will split the audio up into *blobs* (Melodyne's term). These blobs, or notes, are based on pitches and notes found in the track. They are placed in Melodyne's editing pane based on where in the file they occur along with their detected pitches. Editing these blobs is what the Melodyne workflow is all about.

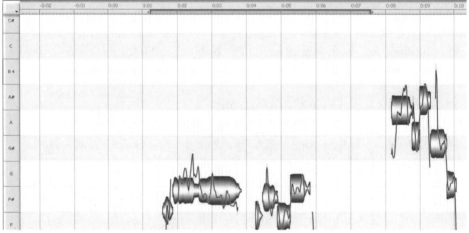

Figure 7.3

THE MELODYNE EDITING ENVIRONMENT

All editing in Melodyne takes place in the large, clean editing pane housing those audio blobs. Across the top horizontal axis of this window is a bar ruler. Here, time is measured in either beats or seconds. Let's take a look at what can be done via the bar ruler.

» Change the time reference of this ruler to different beat divisors or to seconds by right-clicking on it and choosing a different reference or divisor.

» Single-click on the bar ruler to place the playback cursor at that point.

» Double left-click on the bar ruler to start playback at that clicked point.

» Click and slowly drag horizontally inside the bar ruler to scrub the audio inside of Melodyne.

» Click-and-drag horizontally near the bottom of the bar ruler to create a cycle that can be looped by double-clicking inside the cycle. The cycle boundaries can be extended or shortened and the cycle itself moved by clicking-and-dragging. When drawing out a cycle, hold down Alt to ignore the bar ruler's time divisors.

Left-clicking on the downward pointing arrow to the left of the bar ruler and choosing Time Grid from the revealed menu also lets you change time measurements. This same menu also offers Pitch Grid, Scale Editor, and View submenus. Under the Pitch Grid submenu, you can choose how blobs are snapped to notes, as follows:

» **No Snap.** Blobs can be dragged to different pitches freely without snapping to any note on the Pitch Grid.

» **Chromatic Snap.** Blobs will snap to the chromatic notes shown on the pitch ruler and extended across the pitch grid.

» **Scale Snap.** If a specific scale has been selected as described below, blobs will snap only to the notes in that scale.

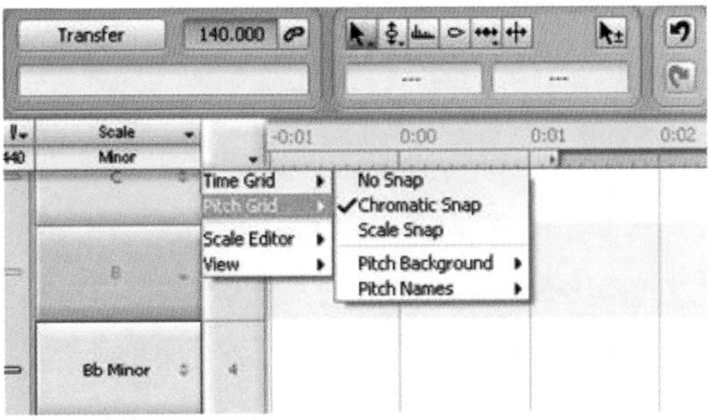

Figure 7.4

MANAGING SCALES AND KEYS IN MELODYNE

On the left-hand vertical axis of the Melodyne editing pane lies a chromatic scale called the pitch ruler.

Right-click anywhere on the pitch ruler and choose the Scale Editor submenu, and from there choose Selection and Master Tuning. This causes two new vertical rulers to appear. The left-most ruler is the reference pitch ruler. By clicking-and-dragging up or down here, you can change the reference pitch from the default A4 = 440 Hz. This acts as a master tuner for the scales and pitches you correct to. Hertz and cents are displayed during dragging to help make this change, which is applied universally. Right-click in this section and choose Standard to return to the 440 Hz default. Here, you can also set the edited reference pitch to be the default.

In between the reference pitch ruler and default pitch ruler is Melodyne's scale ruler. Click on any note in the scale ruler to set it as the tonic (also known as root or key). This opens a menu where you can select the tonic note and define the scale as major or minor (choose Open Scale for more scale options). Tonics appear in boldface print on the scale ruler.

When a new tonic is established, Melodyne does not automatically shift the analyzed pitches (represented as blobs) to reflect this change. You can initiate that change by double-clicking on the note blobs, or by choosing the Notes Reflect Scale Changes submenu when right-clicking on the scale ruler, and then choosing either Tuning or Tuning and Mode.

Melodyne offers flexibility here that extends beyond the scope of this book. Fortunately, they have an extensive video library on their website for those who wish to learn more.

It's worth adding that instead of viewing note names, one can view scale degrees (as in I, IV, V, and so on—based on how far the note is from the tonic). This is great for musicians who often express music in such a way. Simply right-click on the pitch ruler, choose the Pitch Names submenu, and then choose Scale Degrees.

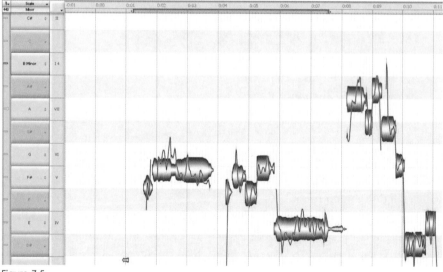

Figure 7.5

MELODYNE'S MYRIAD SCALES

Chromatic, major, and minor scales are always available at the top level in Melodyne by clicking on the scale ruler. Dozens of other scales are available by selecting Open Scale from this same menu. This opens the Open Scale window, where you can choose a scale category and any of the scales within that category. In this window you can then choose a tuning, mode, tonic, and reference pitch for the new scale or the existing one.

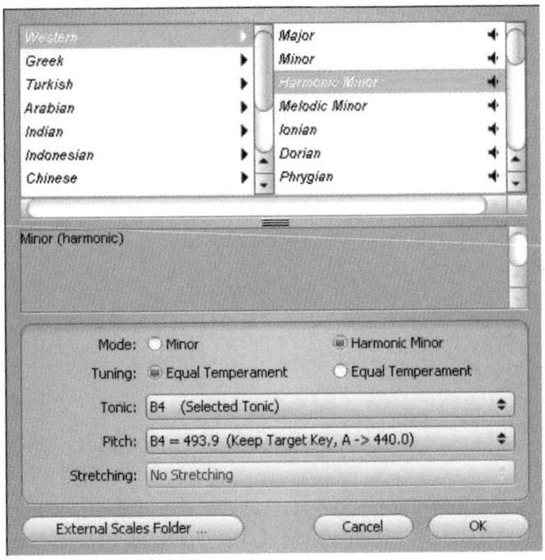

Figure 7.6

MELODYNE'S ALGORITHMS

Melodyne uses different algorithms for monophonic and polyphonic pitch correction. These are available from the Algorithm menu at the top of the Melodyne window. You have three choices:

» **Melodic.** For monophonic material.

» **Percussive.** For rhythmic and percussive material lacking a distinct pitch.

» **Polyphonic.** For polyphonic material.

You can apply these different algorithms to a single audio file after audio transfer. Setting the proper algorithm prior to audio transfer expedites workflow.

NAVIGATING AROUND MELODYNE'S EDITING PANE

Along with the customary scrollbars (scrollers) and zoom buttons on the x- and y-axis of Melodyne's editing pane, there are two powerful tools available for navigation. You can find these tools by right-clicking in the edit window or by clicking-and-holding the Main tool (shown as an arrow cursor) in Melodyne's toolbox.

» **The Scroll tool.** Use this hand-shaped tool to click and move in any direction, to make visible different sections of the tracked audio inside Melodyne's editing pane.

» **The Zoom tool.** Use this magnifying glass–shaped tool to zoom in and out on one or both axes of the edit window. Just click, hold, and drag this cursor in the direction you wish to zoom. Drag diagonally to zoom simultaneously on both axes. Double-clicking on a blob with this tool centers it in the editing pane.

Figure 7.7

Give both of these tools a try to experience how easy they are to use. You can toggle between them by pressing the Control (Windows) or Command (Mac) key.

You can also zoom in or out by clicking-and-dragging the handles on the vertical and horizontal scrollers. This is a fast way to zoom.

To increase or reduce the size of blobs in relation to the editing pane, use the vertical slider near the bottom right of the editing pane.

MONOPHONIC PITCH CORRECTION IN MELODYNE

Melodyne's Melodic algorithm does a great job of detecting pitches in monophonic material. Once this has occurred and Melodyne has placed blobs inside the editing pane based on pitch and time, correcting those pitches involve moving and editing blobs using Melodyne's tools and macros. It's easy and intuitive, and learning how to do it well takes an understanding of the following tools and the workflow they inspire.

MELODYNE'S MAIN TOOL

The Main tool, which uses an arrow for its cursor, changes based on where it is hovering in the editing pane. To help manage this contextual tool, turn on Show Blob Info from the View drop-down menu (it should be on by default). With this on, hovering over any blob will reveal vertical and horizontal dividers within the blob. The Main tool can perform different editing functions based on the Main tool's cursor location within the zones created by these dividers. The Main tool is available from the toolbox or from the editing pane's right-click menu.

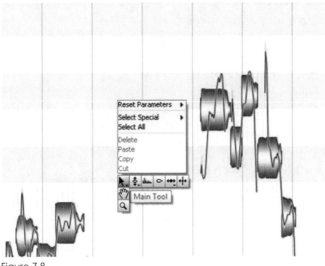

Figure 7.8

The following editing functions are available using the Main tool. Give each a try with the audio you've transferred into Melodyne.

» **Pitch correction.** Use the Main tool to drag a blob up or down to a new pitch. New pitches are auditioned as you move blobs.

» **Note splitting.** Place the Main tool at the top of a blob, then double-click on it to separate it at that click point. You can also double-click on separation markers to heal them. Note separations are shown as gray vertical lines. You can use the Main tool to click-and-drag on these lines to change the split point. Select them from the View menu to see them if they are not already visible.

» **Blob/Note length editing.** Place the Main tool near either end of a blob and click, hold, and drag to extend or shorten its length or change its starting point.

» **Time placement editing.** Click in the center of a blob with the Main tool and drag it horizontally forward or backward in time.

» **Pitch auditioning.** Click-and-hold on a blob to play its associated audio.

» **Blob selection.** Use the Main tool to click and select single blobs, Shift-click to select multiple blobs, or click-and-drag a region to select a group of blobs.

MELODYNE'S PITCH TOOLS

While the Main tool turns into a pitch tool when moving blobs vertically to different pitches, Melodyne also offers dedicated pitch tools for more detailed pitch editing. Pitch tools are available by right-clicking in the editing pane, or from the toolbox at the top of the Melodyne window. Beneath the toolbox, values can be entered into the Inspector for the parameters of the currently selected tool. Experiment with these tools as you read about them below.

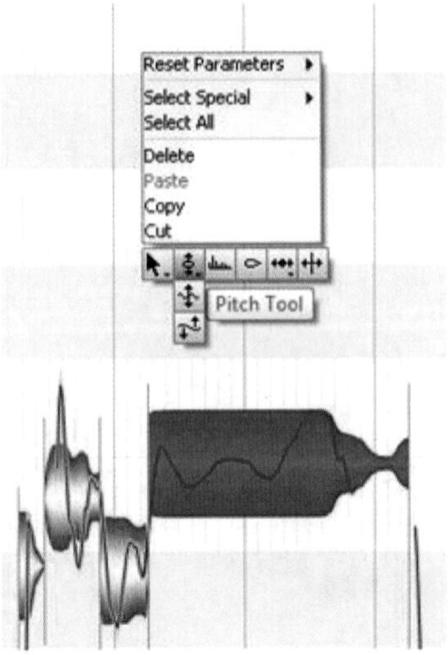

THE PITCH TOOL

This tool does the same job the Main tool does when moving blobs to different pitches. Select it from the toolbox or from the editing

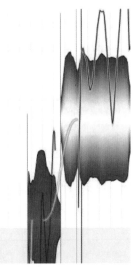

Figure 7.9

pane's right-click menu, and then click on a blob and drag it to the desired pitch. That's how simple professional pitch correction and manipulation is inside the world of Melodyne. Easier still, double-click on a blob to snap it to the closest semitone.

How blobs move when using this tool is based largely on the snap settings established from the pitch ruler's Pitch Grid submenu. You can override those settings by holding down the Alt key when moving blobs.

The original placement of these blobs is based on the average (center) pitch contained in each blob. Even though a blob may be resting perfectly on a note in the pitch grid, its intonation may be less than perfect. Listening more than looking will help reveal this, and Melodyne offers tools (Pitch Drift and Pitch Modulation) to address this. Both are described below.

PITCH TRANSITIONS

When using the Pitch tool, Melodyne shows orange pitch transition curves between notes. Use the Pitch tool to edit the slope (and therefore speed) of that transition by placing it near the start of the orange transition curve and clicking-and-dragging up or down. Double-clicking at this

Figure 7.10

point in the transition curve will remove it. Use this to change the articulation of the performance and edit pitch glides. Double-click again to bring that transition back.

THE PITCH MODULATION TOOL

This pitch subtool is located beneath the Pitch tool from either the toolbox or from the editing pane's right-click menu. Use it for managing vibrato and rapid modulations present in the transferred audio that cause unintended pitchiness or poor intonation. It's also the tool you want when working with pitch correction as an effect.

Inside each blob (and sometimes in between adjacent blobs) are red pitch curves. These curves reflect pitch modulations present in the pitches Melodyne has detected and defined via blobs. These subtle pitch variations or modulations are a natural component of singing. The Pitch Modulation tool allows you to manipulate these modulations in order to tame or accentuate vibrato and reduce pitchiness. Make straight lines out of these curves to achieve the vocal effect.

To use this tool, simply click-and-hold inside a blob, and then drag up or down.

Double-click on these edited blobs to toggle between the pitch curve edits you have made and the original, unaltered curve. This is a great way to A/B your edits against the original audio.

THE PITCH DRIFT TOOL

This subtool, located beneath the Pitch Modulation tool and available from both the editing pane's right-click menu and the toolbox (just click-and-hold on the Pitch tool) is used to tame slower, unintended changes in pitch that are usually the result of a bad or pitchy performance. Whereas the Pitch Modulation tool is designed for handling subtle modulations in pitch, the Pitch Drift tool works on larger, slower modulations that are usually the result of poor technique, often occurring near the end of notes, or near the beginning if the vocalist struggles to find the right note.

Use the Pitch Drift tool to tame these pitchy passages. Click on a blob with it, then hold and drag up or down. Watch those red pitch curves to gain a solid understanding of what this tool is doing, and how it differs from the Pitch Modulation tool. The Pitch Drift tool shifts the curves or portions of the curves up or down to make them more in tune, while the Pitch Modulation tool increases or decreases the width of the pitch modulation itself.

Use the Pitch Drift and Pitch Modulation tools together on blobs that, even though they are on the correct notes, still sound off or poorly intonated. You can hear the results of your edits as they are applied, making these tools quite easy to use.

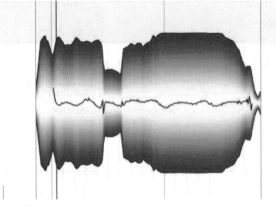

Figure 7.11

THE FORMANT TOOL

Melodyne dedicates a tool for editing formants, those subtle but significant frequencies largely responsible for a vocalist's timbre. This tool is great for managing formants when pitch correction occurs over large intervals. It can also be used to create effects, such as making a female voice sound more male, and vice versa.

Select the Formant tool from either the toolbar or from the editing pane's right-click menu. When selected, thick, orange horizontal bars will appear inside the blobs. These reference the formants for each blob. To edit the formant of a blob (or group of blobs if selected) regardless of where the formant bar is located, click-and-hold inside the blob and drag up or down. The placement of edited formant markers reveals how far the formant has been shifted.

When a formant has been edited, an additional orange line appears

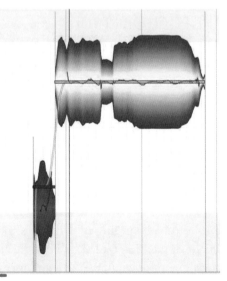

Figure 7.12

showing the formant transition between adjacent notes or pitches. The speed or slope of this transition can be edited by moving this tool to the end of the blob where the formant transition line starts. Here, the cursor will change to a Formant Transition icon. When this icon appears, click-and-drag up or down on the formant transition to change its slope. Double-clicking on a formant transition when this tool is active removes the formant transition altogether. Double-click again to bring it back.

THE AMPLITUDE TOOL

Vocalists often use volume to heighten and convey emotion in their performances. Melodyne's Amplitude tool gives you control over the volume (amplitude) of each blob.

To edit amplitude on a per-blob basis, select this tool from the toolbox or from the editing pane's right-click menu, then click-and-hold on a blob and drag up (increase volume) or down (decrease volume). This tool also works on groups of blogs when selected. Blobs edited with this tool will change their size to reflect the change in amplitude. The meter beneath the Transfer button also shows amplitude changes while using this tool.

To mute a blob, double-click on it with this tool. To unmute it, double-click again. This can be put to great use for stutter types of effects.

When a blob's amplitude has been edited, amplitude transition lines will appear between these blobs. Hovering the cursor to the end of the blob where these transitions begin turns the cursor into the Amplitude Transition tool. Click-and-drag vertically on these transitions to change their slope, and therefore their transition speed. Double-click when this tool is active to remove an amplitude transition altogether. Double-click again to return it.

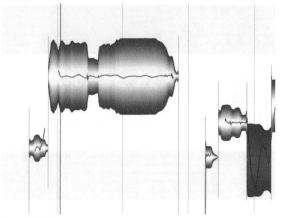

Figure 7.13

THE NOTE SEPARATION TOOL

Breaking up blobs using the Note Separation tool is a key component to Melodyne's editing workflow. The smaller the blob, the greater the editing precision, since it allows editing on smaller and smaller pieces of audio.

Select this tool from the toolbox or from the editing pane's right-click menu, place it over a blob and double-click on it to separate it at the clicked point.

Do not be surprised if one or more of the blobs created by the cut shift to different pitches on the pitch grid. This is because placement of those blobs is based on the average center pitch calculated by Melodyne. Blobs created by the Note Separation tool will have their center pitch recalculated, which could cause them to shift to different semitones.

Vertical lines will appear wherever the Note Separation tool was used. Drag these horizontally to change where a cut was made.

When selecting a blob or group of blobs with his tool, vertical lines will appear at the beginning and end of each blob. These lines can also be dragged horizontally to change start and end points for the selected blobs. This can be put to great use for effect purposes and for editing melody or time in Melodyne.

Double-clicking on a note separation line will remove it and mend the cut. This works on both multiple and single blobs.

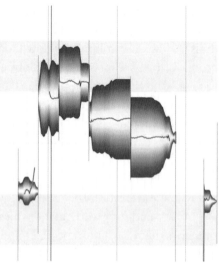

Figure 7.14

ONE-CLICK PITCH CORRECTION WITH MELODYNE'S MACROS

While the Melodyne interface seems tailored for surgical yet speedy pitch and time editing, the program also offers global (macro) tools that can be very effective. On performances that just need a bit of nudging to the correct note, give these tools a try.

THE PITCH MACRO

Melodyne offers two pitch macro controls, available by clicking on the Correct Pitch button on the upper right of the Melodyne window. This opens a small window featuring Correct Pitch Center and Correct Pitch Drift sliders.

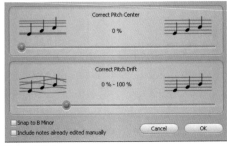

Figure 7.15

» **Correct Pitch Center.** Moving the Correct Pitch Center slider to the right moves all blobs closer to the nearest semitone relative to their detected pitches. At 100% (all the way to the right), blobs are centered on their closest semitone.

If you wish to snap notes to an established tonic and scale, use the Snap to Scale checkbox located at the bottom left of the Pitch Macro window.

Melodyne assumes that your manual edits were intentional and should not be altered by the macro. Therefore, notes (blobs) that have been manually edited to new pitch locations are not affected by this slider unless you have clicked on the checkbox next to "Include notes already edited manually."

» **Correct Pitch Drift.** This slider works on the same types of pitch modulations as the Pitch Drift tool. Using the Correct Pitch Drift slider is a great way to fix pitch-drifting issues, especially when they are pervasive in the performance. The results here are improved intonation without compromising transparent pitch correction. This slider affects all blobs.

Melodyne's pitch macros work on the entire track transferred (or loaded) into the program unless one or more notes or blobs have been selected. These macros can be used at any time during the editing process.

MELODYNE'S REAL-TIME CONTROLS

Melodyne offers three real-time controls: pitch, formant, and amplitude. These are located in the upper right of the Melodyne window. These controls work globally on the track and are ideal for automation. Each knob increases or decreases the parameters they are assigned to. Right-click on any knob to adjust its range.

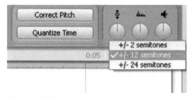

Figure 7.16

POLYPHONIC PITCH CORRECTION IN MELODYNE

Melodyne's DNA (Direct Note Access) allows for pitch correction of polyphonic material. It is geared toward working with single notes within a chord or harmonically complex passage, such as a guitar chord played on an instrument with a string out of tune. It can also be used to change chord voicings and timing.

Polyphonic pitch correction workflow is virtually identical to monophonic pitch correction workflow, with a few additional considerations.

Once polyphonic audio is inside of Melodyne, set its algorithm (from the Algorithm menu) to Polyphonic. This may have been done for you, if, during analysis, Melodyne sufficiently detected polyphonic material in the audio. Under the Algorithm drop-down menu, you can set Polyphonic as the default algorithm if you primarily use Melodyne with polyphonic material.

Once audio has been analyzed using the Polyphonic algorithm, simply use Melodyne's tools to manually move blobs and manipulate their pitch (or time) parameters until you are satisfied with the results (see also the earlier section "Monophonic Pitch Correction in Melodyne" section). In both cases (and this goes for all the programs covered in this book), let your ears be your guide.

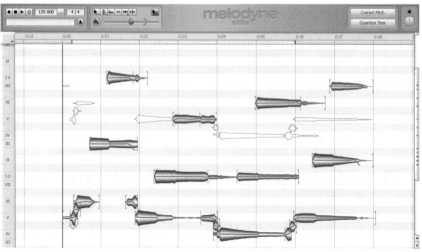

Figure 7.17

NOTE ASSIGNMENT MODE

Melodyne's polyphonic pitch detection algorithm has the difficult job of deciding which pitches are notes played on an instrument and which are overtones from those played notes. Melodyne offers surgical control over this process via Note Assignment mode.

With polyphonic audio inside Melodyne (piano and guitar chords work great), enter Note Assignment mode by clicking on its tool located to the right of Melodyne's toolbox. In this mode, along with the colored blobs that represent pitches available for manipulation, Melodyne also shows clear blobs representing detected overtones of the polyphonic material. Depending on the material, some of these clear blobs may fall on notes and pitches that should be available for editing, and some of the colored blobs may sit on overtones that should not be edited because they are a by-product of a note or pitch, and not the note itself.

Note Assignment mode is only for fine-tuning pitch detection (it is also available for monophonic audio should you need it). It is not an editing environment, and therefore no blobs can be moved when in this mode. You can, however, still cut up blobs in Note Assignment mode, as described below.

Playing back the track in Note Assignment mode while studying the placement of blobs will help determine what changes need to be made for note and overtone blobs. In this mode, double-clicking on a note blob turns it into an overtone blob and vice versa.

Nothing you do in Note Assignment mode changes the actual audio. It only changes what is available for editing by assisting polyphonic pitch detection. Do not be surprised if, in the act of changing blobs in Note Assignment mode, new blobs are created and old ones are moved or removed. This is because the act of identifying notes can affect the overtones that belong to that note, and the act of identifying overtones can affect the notes to which they belong.

THE NOTE ASSIGNMENT SLIDER

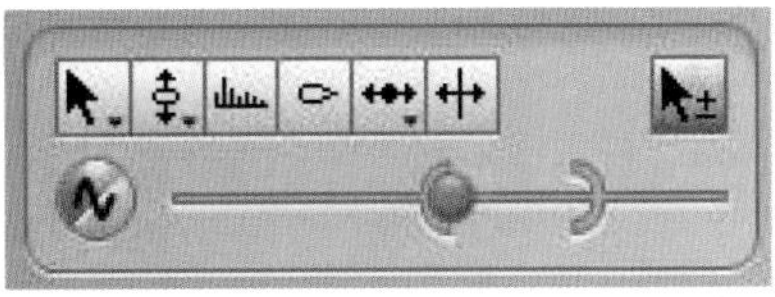

The Note Assignment slider, located beneath the toolbox, helps you manage overtone and note blob creation when you are working with polyphonic audio. This slider contains an orange disc surrounded by two brackets.

Figure 7.18

Dragging the right-hand bracket to the right causes Melodyne to create more overtone blobs; dragging to the left, less. Dragging the orange disc to the right creates more note blobs, and to the left, less. Since you can never have more notes than overtones, dragging the overtone bracket to the left will, at some point, cause the orange note blob disc to also move leftward. Experiment with this to fully understand what is going on here. The goal is to use the slider to get Melodyne to create a quantity of note blobs that closely matches the number of actual notes.

FROM ENERGY TO OVERTONES TO NOTES

During playback of the audio in Melodyne, it's not unusual for notes to be heard in which no blobs (either for overtones or actual notes) are present, even when the Note Assignment slider is all the way to the right (denoting maximum blob creation). To address this, make sure that the Note Assignment slider is set all the way to the right, and then move the cursor around the editing pane, especially around areas where notes were heard but not seen. Doing so causes black ghostly images to appear in the editing pane. Double-click on these to turn them into blobs. Double-click again as needed to turn these into overtones.

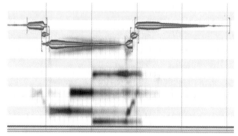

Figure 7.19

NOTE SEPARATION IN NOTE ASSIGNMENT MODE

While in detection mode, you can also add, remove, or move note separators that may have been placed incorrectly by Melodyne. If you do not see the note separators, select that option from the View menu. While in Note Assignment mode, the cursor will turn into the Note Separation tool when hovering near the top of a note blob. Once again, the secret here is to listen and watch, and make your cuts where different pitches occur under the same blob.

In Note Assignment mode, create a satisfactory polyphonic editing environment by performing the following:

>> Make sure all notes have properly received a colored blob.

>> Make sure all clear blobs are placed only on overtones.

>> Make sure all colored blobs are broken down into individual pitches or notes.

Keep in mind that in Melodyne's editing mode, those overtone blobs will be hidden and unavailable.

MELODYNE'S VENETIAN BLINDS

At the top and bottom of Melodyne's edit window are "venetian blinds" used for limiting the range of frequencies available for manipulation (you may need to scroll to view these). If you see overtones or notes that you know are not part of the polyphonic material, click-and-drag the blinds over them, thus limiting the range of available blobs within the program. All blobs obscured by these blinds will be unavailable when you return to editing mode unless you manually select them.

Whenever you enter Note Assignment mode, be advised that your undo history will be deleted. Because of this, the detection and assignment part of your workflow should occur before you begin editing.

MELODYNE'S UNDO SYSTEM

Along with Melodyne's global undo and redo feature available from the edit menu, a suite of specific undos or resets are also available whenever you have selected a blob or group of blobs that have received edits. For specific pitch edit undos, right-click and choose Reset Pitch Parameters, and then select the parameter you wish to reset. You can also click on the edit menu and choose Reset Specific Edits, and then choose the appropriate submenu.

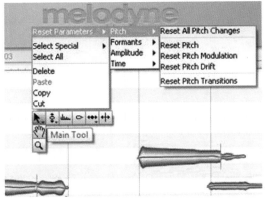

Figure 7.20

8 PITCH CORRECTION TIPS AND TRICKS

The following tips and tricks can be applied equally to each software plug-in covered here, with excellent results.

RECORDING VOCALS FOR PITCH CORRECTION

Figure 8.1

Pitch correction cannot happen without the technology first detecting the pitches found in the source audio. Recording vocal tracks with effects will impede this critical step in the process. That alone should convince you to record your vocals dry as burnt toast, while giving the vocalist as much sonic goop as he or she wants in their headphone mix, as long as it helps him or her nail the part. EQ, compressors, and de-essors in front of a pitch correction plug-in can sometimes benefit pitch processing, unless the EQ or compression boosts unmusical noises in the track. A typical signal chain for vocals that includes pitch correction looks something like this:

Users of iZotope's Nectar have the benefit of the plug-in containing everything needed for a vocal track in the right order. So a single instance of Nectar on a vocal track may be all you need.

Vocals should nearly always be recorded in mono, and therefore mono instances of pitch correction plug-ins should be used. When they have been recorded in stereo, be sure to use stereo instances of the plug-in.

REAL-TIME PITCH CORRECTION REQUIREMENTS

The requirements for effective real-time pitch correction are fairly straight-forward:

» **A clean vocal track.** Having few or no noises in the vocal is ideal in general, and when they exist they can interfere with pitch detection. Use your DAW's waveform editing tools to remove as much noise from the vocal track as possible. Adjusting pitch detection tracking settings can also help when noises have been detected as valid pitches.

» **The vocal part does not stray far from the correct pitch.** The rule of thumb is that the farther away the part is from the correct pitch, the easier it is for the pitch correction process to be heard, especially when you are working in real-time mode. Many of the plug-ins covered here offer parameters to handle this.

» **Vibrato and other vocal techniques are not extreme.** Pitch correction algorithms can sometimes break a vibrato or vocal technique into multiple corrected pitches. While this can be good when working with effects, it's generally bad for transparent pitch correction. Most of the titles covered in this book offer parameters to manage this, and you may find it easier to work in offline mode whenever vibrato or vocal techniques are so extreme or pitchy that they cause real-time pitch correction processing to sound, well, processed.

TRANSPARENT PITCH CORRECTION TIPS

Transparent pitch correction is mandatory for many forms of music. The goal here is for the vocal to sound naturally in tune and not pitch processed. Here are some tips on how to master this.

» **There is no substitute for a great performance.** Getting the best performance out of the vocalist should be the primary goal of any producer or audio engineer. When the singer shines, so does the project. Your vocal tracks should be a composite of the best takes. Record as many as needed (within reason) to accomplish this.

When pitch problems aren't discovered until the mixing phase of the project, using pitch correction tools is usually far easier, faster, and better than calling a vocalist back for another tracking session.

» **Art is imperfect.** The best singers emote their way through a performance. And therefore, they are not always perfectly on pitch. Apply pitch correction with great discretion and subtlety to let the nuances of the performance shine through. Not every variance in pitch requires correction. Listen with your ears and your heart when applying pitch correction. Parameters such as Humanize (Auto-Tune), Correction Strength (Nectar), Ratio and Note Transition (Waves Tune), and Pitch Modulation and Drift tools (Melodyne) all help preserve and manage the natural imperfections that make singing sound human and not robotic.

» **Choose precision over blunt force.** The pitch correction requirements of a screaming chorus will be quite different than those of a quiet breakdown. Apply pitch correction to suit the part as well as the performance. Graphical/offline pitch correction dominates because it offers a unique set of pitch parameters for each note. This is key to achieving highly professional results.

» **Use formant control.** This option should almost always be left on since without it, it's too easy for pitch correction to sound obvious and unnatural.

» **Keep it chromatic.** Using a chromatic scale for real-time pitch correction and for correction/retune speeds between 20 ms and 75 ms can be enough to gently nudge the vocal to the correct notes. This is both a subtle and effective approach for vocals that are only mildly to moderately pitchy.

» **Speed kills.** The principal parameter for pitch correction is the speed at which correction is applied. Both the part and the pitchiness dictate how to set this important parameter. When transparent pitch correction starts becoming apparent, this parameter is often to blame. Automating correction/retune speeds for real-time pitch correction (fast for short notes, slower for longer notes) is easy to do and can benefit transparent real-time pitch correction.

» **Listen.** All these wonderful knobs and sliders and blobs and curves don't amount to a hill of beans if you don't listen closely to the part and what you are doing to it.

Remember—the results of properly set transparent pitch correction are simply vocals that sound as though they were originally sung in tune.

PITCH CORRECTION EFFECT TIPS

Achieving pitch correction as a vocal effect is astonishingly easy to do. The key to doing it well is setting it to fit the singer and the song without making it sound generic. Here are some tips to help you master it.

> » **Speed is killer.** The same correction speed or retune speed parameters that are key to transparent pitch correction are also key to achieving the vocal effect. But in this case, you want it fast in order to maximize *pitch quantization* (the technical term for this effect). The goal here is to remove natural pitch modulations and make pitch curves and contours as flat as possible. Start at the fastest setting (0 ms) and turn off any humanization settings. Start heavy and scale back as needed to fit the song and the part.

> » **The greater the difference between source pitch and output pitch, the stronger the effect.** Keep this in mind when tracking, since singing in keys and octaves that are different from that of the final mix can help (it's easy enough to transpose electronic music to help the vocalist accomplish this). Then use key and scale settings to put the vocal back into the right key. Graphical mode pitch correction shines here by letting you move correction objects to different pitches far away from the original.

> » **Melody matters.** The effect lends itself to melody manipulation, and often requires it to help create large intervals between source and output pitch. Use manual pitch correction to create a custom melody. You do not need a lot of notes—just a few of the right ones at various lengths. Experiment and take advantage of those undo and redo buttons.

> » **Static is not dramatic.** Use automation in real-time mode, or take advantage of per-object settings in offline mode to change correction speeds for different parts in the track to keep it dynamic.

The titles covered in this book are all great production tools in their own right. It's quite common to own more than one, much the way studios and hobbyists own more than one reverb, guitar, or compressor. Try demo versions of the software to see which ones best fit your music-production environment.

APPENDIX: ABOUT THE DVD-ROM

The DVD-ROM contains tutorials for each of the pitch correction titles covered in *Pitch Correction Software Now!* These videos include tips and tricks that will help users achieve professional, transparent pitch correction results and popular pitch correction effects using each of the software titles covered in this book.

1. Auto-Tune Effect and Standard Pitch Correction Using Auto-Tune EFX 2

2. Mixing Effect and Transparent Correction Using Graphical Mode's Line Objects and Note Objects

3. MIDI and the Auto-Tune Effect in Auto-Tune Live

4. Using Melodyne Editor for Effect and Transparent Pitch Correction

5. Automatic Pitch Correction in Nectar

6. Using Nectar Manual Pitch Correction for Pitch Correction Effects and Melody Work

7. Using The T-Pain Effect for Standard (Transparent) Pitch Correction and T-Pain-Style Vocal Effects

8. Effect and Transparent Pitch Correction with Waves Tune

INDEX